THE ENGLISH GRADUAL

PART I

THE PLAINCHANT OF THE ORDINARY

Edited by
FRANCIS BURGESS
Musical Director of the Gregorian Association

THE PLAINCHANT PUBLICATIONS COMMITTEE
61 THE RIDGE, HASTINGS,
EAST SUSSEX, TN34 2AB

First Edition	-	-	1871
Second Edition	-	-	1920
Third Edition	-	-	1933
Fourth Edition	-	-	1942
Fifth Edition	-	-	1949
Sixth Edition	-	-	1955
Seventh Edition	-	-	1977
Eighth Edition	-	-	1982

Printed in England by John Blackburn Ltd
Old Run Road, Leeds 10

PREFACE

The first edition of THE ENGLISH GRADUAL was published by the Gregorian Association in 1871 under the editorship of the Reverend S. S. Greatheed. It contained a number of Plainchant settings of the various parts of the English Communion Office and, by comparison with its contemporary publications and in the light of such information as was then available, it exhibited an advanced standard of Plainsong scholarship for nearly a quarter of a century.

But now we are living in a changed world. The researches of the Benedictines of Solesmes have revealed the weaknesses of the evidence upon which English Plainsong scholars were wont to rely in the nineteenth century. The "typical editions" of the Vatican Commissioners on the Sacred Chant have confirmed and completed the labours of Solesmes, and the methods of Plainsong technique advocated in the works of Dom Gueranger and Dom Pothier now receive the highest official approbation, to the confusion of all corrupt and mutilated versions of the Chant of which that of Ratisbon is, perhaps, the most characteristic. In England, the publications of the Plainsong and Mediæval Music Society, based upon the Solesmes technique but confined, for the most part, to those versions of the Chant found in the Salisbury MSS, have made a contribution to musico-liturgical scholarship in the English Church, of which the more venerable Gregorian Association has not been slow to avail itself in its later years.

The purpose of the present issue of THE ENGLISH GRADUAL, as now revised and enlarged, is to provide the clergy, and their choirs and congregations, with a simple, accurate and easily understood manual of Plainchant for use at the Consecration of the Eucharist. To this end modern notation has been utilised to serve as an exact transcription of the manner in which the Plainchant should be rendered by the voices. The ordinary note, or note-group, in the Plainchant is represented by one or more quavers. When the rhythm of the text or of the melody requires that a note shall be *slightly* broadened and lengthened, the quaver has a short horizontal line placed over it. Those notes or note-groups which require lengthening to *nearly double* their normal duration are represented by crotchets instead of quavers. The addition of the *sol-fa* characters over the ordinary staff of five lines may be found of use when the melodies are being learned for the first time.

It may be desirable at this point to deal with the general arrangement of the melodies contained in this volume. The plan adopted has been to set out the *Kyrie eleison, Sanctus, Agnus Dei* and *Gloria in excelsis* (but not the *Credo*) in groups for performance. Each group of melodies bears a distinguishing number and it will usually be convenient for the grouping to be adhered to in practical use. When desired, however, any melody may be transferred from one group to another. The group of melodies numbered IV (on Double Feasts) is the already well-known and much-loved *Missa de Angelis*, of which there have been many English adaptations since the dawn of the Catholic Revival. For the sake of completeness its own *Sanctus* and *Agnus Dei* have been included even though these are omitted in many recent editions. Those who are inclined to regard this group of melodies as being of foreign origin will be interested to note the following *Benedicamus* Tones in the Salisbury Antiphoner:

Be- ne- di- ca- mus do- mi- no.

Be- ne- di- ca- mus do- mi- no.

which bear so striking a resemblance to the *Kyrie de Angelis* that the similarity can hardly have been a matter of chance. It will also be useful to compare it with the *Agnus Dei* in Group VII. This melody is found in the York Gradual, and though its likeness with the *de Angelis* theme is not so striking as in the Sarum example cited above, there is nevertheless, a strong family resemblance.

Of the eight *Credo* melodies given, any one of these may be used whenever the *Credo* is recited. *Credo ii* is that given in the Sarum Gradual and done into English by the Plainsong and Mediæval Music Society. *Credo iii* is the *de Angelis* melody, and the fourth setting is that known as *cardinalis*, generally ascribed to the fifteenth century. The present adaptation of this melody is, for the most part, the work of Dr. Palmer. *Credo v* is a thirteenth century form which has survived among the Benedictines; *Credo vii* is the traditional Ambrosian setting, which should be sung by two bodies of voices, as marked. *Credo vi* is the well-known setting by John Merbecke. In this, as well as in the rest of Merbecke's melodies in Group XV, Mr. Wyatt's accurate and widely used version has been followed.

Plainchant is most effective when it is sung antiphonally, either between Cantors and Choir (with the Congregation), or between Men and Boys, or between two sides of the Choir if it consist entirely of men or entirely of boys.

The following rules should be observed:

In *Kyrie eleison* the Cantors intone the first verse up to the asterisk (*), at which point the Choir will take up the melody and complete the first clause. The verses are then continued antiphonally up to the ninth clause, that verse being begun by the Cantors up to the single asterisk, at which point it is taken up by the Choir. In certain of the more ornate Kyries the concluding verse has a single asterisk near the beginning and a double asterisk further on. In these cases the Cantors sing up to the first asterisk, the Choir continue to the second asterisk, and from that point it is sung full to the end.

The *Credo* is intoned by the Celebrant and thereafter should be sung full throughout, without antiphony, except in the case of the Ambrosian setting.

The *Sanctus* is intoned by the Cantors up to the asterisk (*) and continued full to the end.

Each verse of *Agnus Dei* is intoned by the Cantors up to the asterisk (*) and continued full.

The *Gloria in excelsis* is intoned by the Celebrant to the first double bar. It is then continued by the Choir to the next double bar, after which it should be sung antiphonally between Cantors and Choir up to the concluding words, which are sung full.

Where there are no Cantors the parts assigned to them above may be taken by one side of the Choir.

In the Choir Responses given at the end an attempt has been made to provide for such additions to the present English Rite as are becoming customary. It will be seen, however, that by the simple process of omitting such Responses as are not required, the existing use of any church may be maintained.

It remains for the Editor to acknowledge his indebtedness to those who have assisted him in the compilation of this work. First and foremost, his grateful thanks are due to the late Dr. Palmer, whose generous advice, based upon long experience, solved many difficulties. To the late Mr. Thomas P. Holmes is due most of the credit for evolving, with his singers at St. Stephen's, Guernsey, a version of *Missa de Angelis* which retains much of the rhythmical simplicity of the original. The courtesy of the Plainsong and Mediæval Music Society must be acknowledged for permitting their existing adaptation of the *Credo* melody to be included, and thanks are also due to the Proprietors of *The English Hymnal* for permission to include the version of the text of the *Dies irae* given in their book. Finally, the Editor would take the opportunity of thanking the Men's Choir of the Gregorian Association for their patience in testing some of these adaptations in manuscript, and he is grateful to Mr. George C. Underwood for his help in the correction of proofs.

A Simple Setting of

VIDI AQUAM

Mode VI

d r-m m-d-r r-d d d d-t l-s s d r-m r-d D
I be - held wa - ter* which pro - ceed-ed from the tem-ple,
d r-m m-s-m r-d r-d D d-r-m d-r r-d D d m-s s s
on the right side there-of, al - le - lu - ya: and all they to
s m-r s m-r s-l-S m s-l-s-s-m m d d-r R d d-t l-s
whom that wa-ter came were heal - ed ev-ery one, and they say,
d-r-m d-r r-d D d-r-m d-r r-d D - d-r-m s-m-m-r-d-R - D
al - le - lu - ya, al - le - lu - ya.
d-r r-d r-m m m m m r f m r d d r-m m-s
Ps. O give thanks un-to the Lord, for he is gra-cious:* and his mer -
r d r d-l d R D d-r r-d r-m M - M r f
-cy en-du-reth for ev - er. Glo - ry be to the Father, and to
and to the Son,
m r d D d r-m M-M m m r f m r d
the Ho-ly Ghost:* As it was in the is now, and ev-er shall be:
beginning,
d r d-l d R D d r-m m-d-r
world with-out end. A - men. I be - held etc.

Versicles on p. 16

INDEX

Asperges me

On all Sundays in the year except in Eastertide

SETTING 1 MODE VII

s - l d - t - l t - d R m - f - s - s - f m - r m r - d
Thou shalt púrge me, * O Lórd, with hýs -
t - d r - d - l t s s - l - s S s - l d - t - l t - d R
- sop, and I shall be cléan: thou shalt wásh me,
r - m - f - m - r d - t l d t - d r - d - l - t s - l - s S
and I shall be whí - ter than snów.
s - d - t d - r r r r - f m m - r R - M r - t d - r r - m - f
Ps. 51. Have mér - cy up - ón me, O Gód: * áf - ter thý
r d - d - d L - S s - d - t d - r r r r r r r r r R
great góod - ness. Gló - ry be to the Fá-ther, and to the Són,
r r - f m m m - r R - M r - t d - r r r r r r r r r
and to the Hó - ly Ghóst: * As it wás in the be-gínning, is nów,
r r - f m m - r R - M r - t d - r r - m - f R d - d - d L - S
and év - er shéll be: wórld with - óut énd. A - men.

Repeat Antiphon Thou shalt purge me.

¶ *On Passion Sunday and Palm Sunday* Glory be *is not sung, but the Psalm* Have mercy *is followed immediately by the Antiphon* Thou shalt purge me.

D - D *L* *D*

℣. O Lórd, shew thy mércy up - - - - ón us.
℟. And gránt us thy salvá - - - - - tion.
℣. O Lórd, héar my práyer.
℟. And lét my crý come ún - - - - - - to thée
℣. The Lórd be wíth you.
℟. And with thy spí - - - - - - - - - rit.

Let us pray **Collect.**

Graciously hear us, O Lord holy, Father almighty, everlasting God: and vouchsafe to send thy holy Angel from heaven; to guard and cherish, to protect and visit, and to defend all who dwell in this thy holy habitation. Through Christ our Lord.

T *D*

℟. A - men.

Setting 2 Another melody *ad libitum* **Mode VII**

s - l d - t d - r R m - m - f m r m r - d t - d r - d l

Thou shalt púrge me,* O Lórd, with hýs-sop, and Í shall

s S s - l d - t d - r R r - m d d - l d t - d r - d l - s S

be cléan: thou shalt wásh me, and Í shall be whí - ter than snów.

Ps. Have mercy, *and Versicles, etc., as above.*

Setting 3 Another melody *ad libitum* **Mode IV**

f f f - m - r M m s - l l - ta l s - f s s - l s - f m - f

Thou shalt púrge me,* O Lórd, with hýs - sop, and Í shall be

M - R d - r f - m f - s S s l ta l s s - f s - l s - f - m M

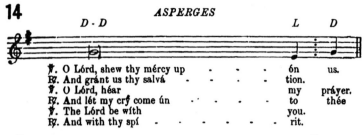

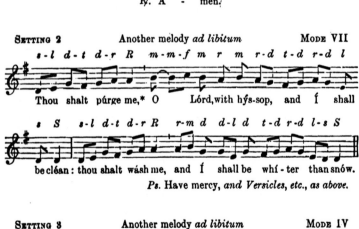

cléan: thou shalt wásh me, and Í shall be whí - ter than snów.

l s-l l l l s l T l s l t-l s-f M l s-l

Ps. 51. Have mér-cy up-ón me, O Gód: * áf-ter thý great góodness. Gló-ry

l l l l l l l l L l l l s l T l s-l l l

be to the Fáther, and to the Són and to the Hóly Ghóst: * As it wás in

l l l l l l l s l T L l s l t-l s-f M

the be-gínning, is nów, and éver shåll be: wórld withóut énd. A - men.

Repeat Antiphon Thou shalt purge me.

Versicles and Collect as above.

VIDI AQUAM

SETTING 4 MODE VIII

On Sundays from Easter Day to Pentecost inclusive

s s-l l-f-l-s s-l-s S s s-l-d-t t-l d-d l-t

I be - héld wá - ter * which pro - céed - ed from

s-l s-d-d-r-l l-s-l-t-L. s s-l s-d-d-r l-s l-d-s-l

the tém - - ple, on the right síde there -

S - F s s-l-f-s s-l-d-l-t L - S s-l s-l-t-d

- - óf, al - le - - lú - - ya: and áll

d t-l t-d t d-d-d-t l-r d-t-d-r-d-t-d-t-l-s-L-S

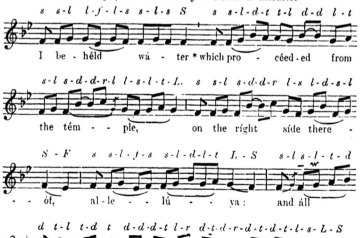

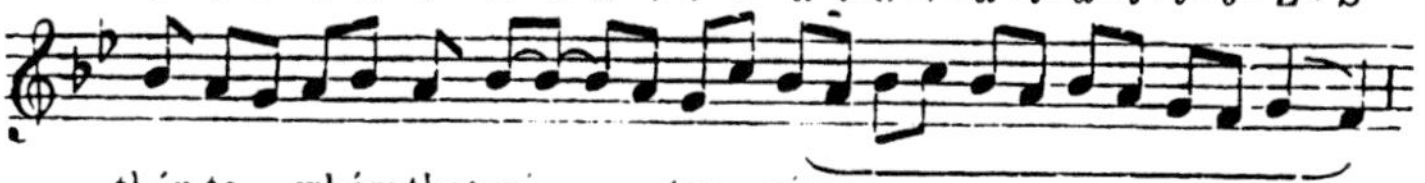

théy to whóm that wá - ter came

were héal - ed év - - ery óne, and they sáy,
al - le - lú - ya, al - le - - - - lú - ya.
Ps. 118. O give thánks un-to the Lórd, for hé is grá-cious: * and his
mér-cy en - dú - reth for év - er. Gló - ry be to the Fáther, and
to the Són, and to the Hó - ly Ghóst. * As it wás in the begínning,
is nów, and év - er shall be: wórld with - óut énd. A - men.

Repeat Antiphon I beheld water.

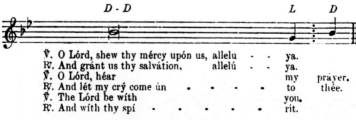

℣. O Lórd, shew thy mércy upón us, allelu - - ya.
℟. And gránt us thy salvátion, allelú - - ya.
℣. O Lórd, héar my práyer.
℟. And lét my crý come ún . . . . . to thée.
℣. The Lórd be wíth you.
℟. And wíth thy spí . . . . . . rit.

COLLECT as on page 4.

I– IN EASTER-TIDE

Lux et origo

Mode VIII

10th century

♪ = 144
s - l - t l l - d - d - t - s l - s - f - s s M
(1.2.3.) *Kýrie* *e - lé-i-son.*
Lórd, *have mér - cy.
d - r - d t - l - D l - d - t s - f - L l - t d - t - l - s
(4.5.6.) *Chríste e -*
Chríst, have
m f S S - t - d - r - d r - m - r - R - T
- lé-i-son. (7.8.) *Ký - - ri - e*
mér - cy. Lórd,
r - d - t - l - s l - t - l l S T l - s S - t - d - r - d
e - lé - i-son. (9) *Ký-ri - e*
have mér - cy. Lórd,
r - m - r - R - T r - d t - l - s l - t - l l S
**e - lé - i-son.*
*have mér - cy.

Sanctus

Mode IV 11th century

♪ = 132
d-r-f f-m-R s-f-s S m-r-m f-m-r-M
Hó - ly, *Hó - ly, Hó - ly
r-m-s m-r f-m M r m s-l-d
Lórd Gód of hósts. Héa-ven and
l-s-f s-l s-f-M s-f m-f-s f-m-r R
éarth are fúll of thy gló - ry.
m f-s s f s m-r f f-m M
Gló - ry be to thée, O Lórd most hígh.
r m s-l-d L l l-s l-d s f-m f-s
Bléss-ed is hé that cóm - eth in the náme
f m-r R m f-s s f s m-r-f-f-m M
of the Lórd. Ho-sán-na in the hígh - est.

Agnus Dei

Mode IV 10th century

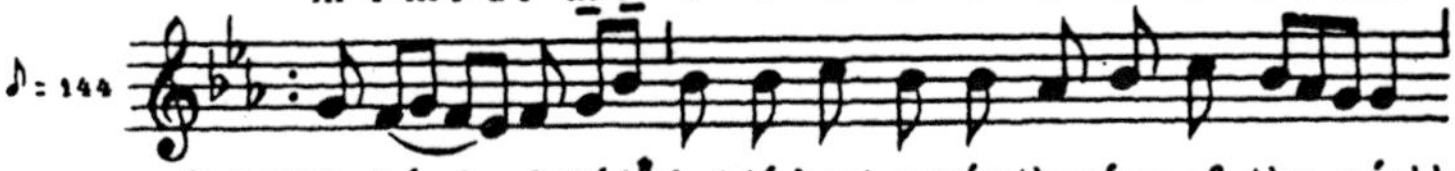
m r-m-r-d r m-s s s l s s f s l s-f-m M
♪= 144
(1.2.3.)O Lámb of Gód,* that tá-kest a-wáy the sins of the wórld:

first and second verses:

d - r - f m - f - r - r - d M s - l - s - f - s s - f - m M
have mér - cy up - ón us.

third verse:

d - r - f m - f - r - r - d - M s - l - s - f - s - s - f - m M
gránt us thy péace.

Gloria in excelsis

Mode I 13th century

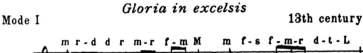

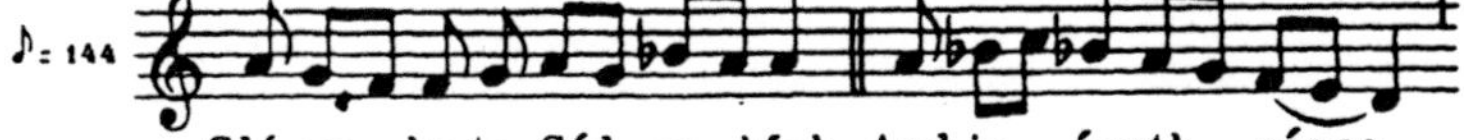
m r - d d r m - r f - m M m f - s f - m - r d - t - L
♪= 144
Gló-ry be to Gód on hígh, And in éarth péace,

s l d r - d - t - d L m - f - m R M s l - s - l M
good-wíll to-wárds mén. We práise thee. We bléss thee.

r m f - s F - M s - l d t - l s - l M
We wór - ship thee. We gló - ri - fy thee.
s m r m l - s d - r r - m - r - d t - l s - l L
We give thánks to thée for thý great gló - ry.
d r - m M s r - d r - m M l s - l l r
O Lórd Gód héa - ven - ly Kíng, Gód the Fá-ther
m - f - s - l s - f - m M m - f - s s - f - m - f r d r
Al - mígh - ty. O Lórd, the ón - ly
d t l - s l - d r - d t - d L m r - d r - m
be - gót - ten Són, Jé - su Chríst. O Lórd Gód,
s - r - d r - m M l - s - l r m - f - s L s - f - M
Lámb of Gód, Són of the Fá - ther.
m f - s s f - m f r - d m r f M
That tá - kest a - wáy the síns of the wórld,

d t - l s - l t - d L L m m f - s s f - m f
have mér - cy up - ón us. [Thou that tá - kest a - wáy
r - d m r f M d t - l s - l t - d L L
the síns of the wórld, have mér - cy up - ón us.]
m m f - s s f - m f r - d m r f M
Thou that tá - kest a - wáy the síns of the wórld,
l - s f - m r M m r - m d d m f
re - céive our práyer. Thou that sít - est at the
s s f - m r r m - r - m L d t l
ríght hánd of Gód the Fá - ther, have mér - cy
s - l - t - d L L m f - s s f - m r F M
up - ón us. For thou ón - ly art hó - ly.
l s l f - m r - m M m s l d t l S - L
Thou ón - ly árt the Lórd. Thou ón - ly, O Je - su Chríst,
O______ Chríst,

(Full)
l-s m f-r d-t-d L d-r l-d-t L-S d r-m
with the Hó - ly Ghóst, art móst high in the

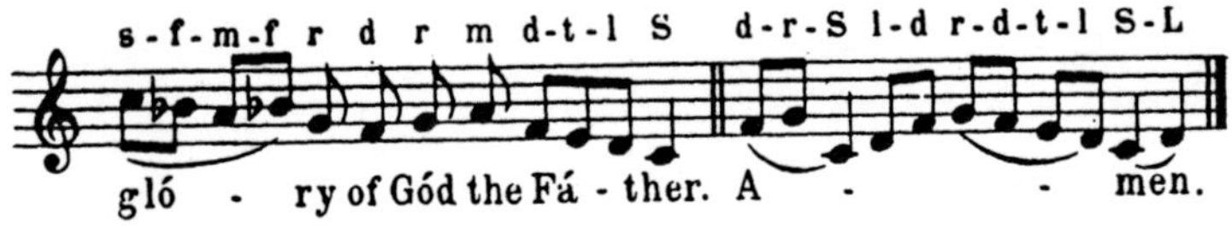
s-f-m-f r d r m d-t-l S d-r-S l-d r-d-t-l S-L
gló - ry of Gód the Fá - ther. A - - men.

Ite, missa est

(a) from Holy Saturday until the Saturday after Easter:

s s s l s f s-l L l s-d-t-l-s f-s-l L-S
℟. Thánks be to Gód, al - le - lú - ia, al-le - - lú - ia.

(b) from Low Sunday until the Saturday in Whitsun-week:

s t-d-r d-r-m-r-R-T r-d-t-l-s l-t-l l S
℟. Thánks be to God.

II On Solemn Feasts

Firmator sancte

Mode VI

13th century

♪ = 144
d l - d D r - m f - m - r - d d l t D
Ký - ri - e *e - lé - i - son.
(1.2.3.) Lórd, * have mér - cy.
d - s s - f - m f - s - l S - M f - m - r - d d l t D
Chrí - ste e - lé - i - son.
(4.5.6.) Chríst, have mér - cy.
d - s s l - s d - t - l - S f - s - l S - M f - m - r - d
Ký - ri - e
(7.8.) Lórd,
d l t D d - s s l - s d - t - l - S
e - lé - i - son. (9) Ký - ri - e
have mér - cy. Lórd,
f - s - l S - M s - f - s - l S - M f - m - r - d d l t D
* e - lé - i - son.
* have mér - cy.

Sanctus

Mode III 11th century

♪ = 132
d d-t-L t-d-r T d l-s l-t t-d-l-s-f
Hó-ly, * Hó - ly, Hó-ly Lórd Gód
s-l-s-f M m m-r s s-l-t d-t-l-t L-S
of hósts. Héaven and éarth are fúll
d l-s l-d-l T t-d-r r d-t t s-l-t d-l S-F
of thy gló - ry. Gló - ry be to thée,
s s-l-s m-r-m M m m-r s l-d d d-t l
O Lórd most hígh. Bléssed is hé that cóm-eth
l l t-d-r-r-d-t l-s l-t T d-t s-l-t d-l-s
in the náme of the Lórd. Ho - -
s m-f-s-s-f-m-R r-l l-s l-d-s l-s-f-r-m M
-sán-na in the hígh - - est.

Agnus Dei

Mode VI **13th century**

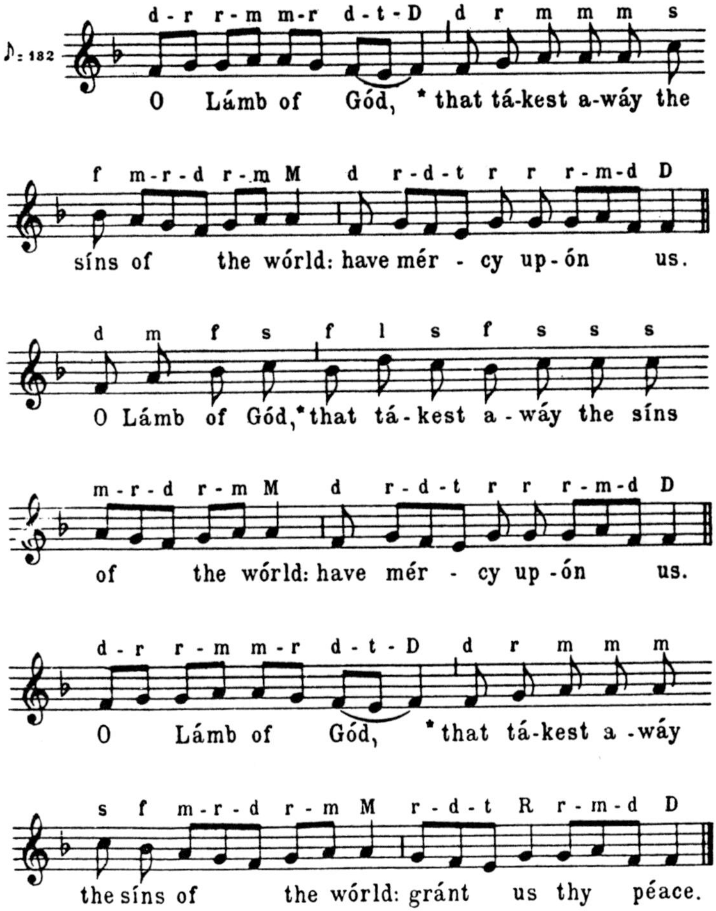
♪: 182
d - r r - m m - r d - t - D d r m m m s
O Lámb of Gód, * that tá-kest a-wáy the
f m - r - d r - m M d r - d - t r r r - m - d D
síns of the wórld: have mér - cy up - ón us.
d m f s f l s f s s s
O Lámb of Gód,* that tá - kest a - wáy the síns
m - r - d r - m M d r - d - t r r r - m - d D
of the wórld: have mér - cy up - ón us.
d - r r - m m - r d - t - D d r m m m
O Lámb of Gód, * that tá-kest a -wáy
s f m - r - d r - m M r - d - t R r - m - d D
the síns of the wórld: gránt us thy péace.

Gloria in excelsis

Mode VIII 10th century

f-s-l f-s s s-l l-t l-s S s s-l l-s f-s
Gló - ry be to Gód on hígh, And in éarth péace,
s s-f m f-s S s-l l-t L-S s-l l-t L-S
good-wíll towárds mén. We práise thee. We bléss thee.
s s-l l-t L-S s-d-t d-r d-t l-d-d-t-s l-f-S
We wór-ship thee. We gló-ri - fy thee.
s s-l l-t l s s-l l-s-s-f m-f S S
We give thánks to thée for thý great gló-ry.
s-f-m r-m-f-s S-L l s s F l-s s
O Lórd Gód, héa-ven-ly Kíng, Gód the
s-d-d-t l-s f-m f-s S s-f-m r-m-f-s s s-l l
Fá - ther Al-mígh-ty. O Lórd the ón-ly
s s f F l-s-f-m f-s S s-l l-t-l L-S
be-gót-ten Són, Jé - su Chríst. O Lórd Gód,

s - l l - t - l L - S s - l l l - t L S
Lámb of Gód, Són of the Fá - ther.
l l - s s s f l - d d - t l t l - s
That tá - kest a - wáy the síns of the wórld,
l - s f m f - s S S l l l - s s s f
have mér - cy up - ón us. [Thou that tá - kest a - wáy
l - d d - t l t l - s l - s f m f - s S S
the síns of the wórld, have mér - cy up - ón us.]
s s s - l - d - l l l l - s s f - m f s s - f - m r - m - f - s
Thou that tá - kest a - wáy the síns of the wórld,
l - d d - t - l - l - s - f s - l S s s s - l - d - l l
re - céive our práyer. Thou that sít - test
l l l - s f m f s s - f - r m - f - s - l l - s
at the ríght hánd of Gód the Fá - ther, have
f m f - s S S s s - l l - t l l - t L S
mér - cy up - ón us. For thou ón - ly art hó - ly,

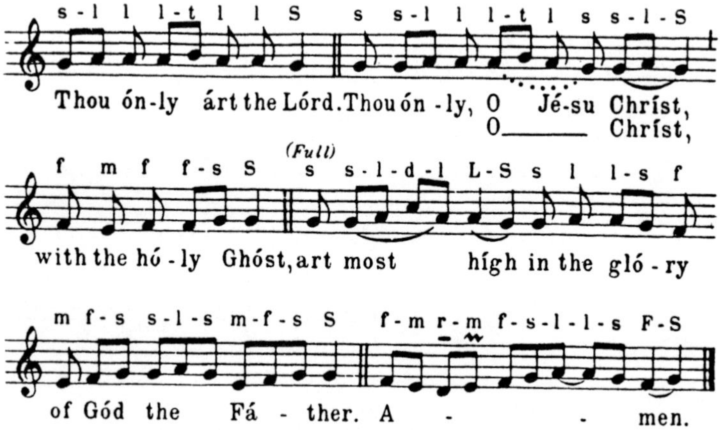
s - l l l - t l l S s s - l l l - t l s s - l - S
Thou ón-ly árt the Lórd. Thou ón - ly, O Jé-su Chríst,
O Chríst,
(Full)
f m f f - s S s s - l - d - l L - S s l l - s f
with the hó - ly Ghóst, art most hígh in the gló - ry
m f - s s - l - s m - f - s S f - m r - m f - s - l - l - s F - S
of Gód the Fá - ther. A - - men.

Ite, missa est

d - t - s - l - S m - f - s - s r - m - r - D d - t - s - l - S
℟. Thánks
m - f - s - s r - m - r - D d - r - m f - m r - d D
be to God.

III.—On Double Feasts

Magnae Deus potentiae

Mode VIII

13th century

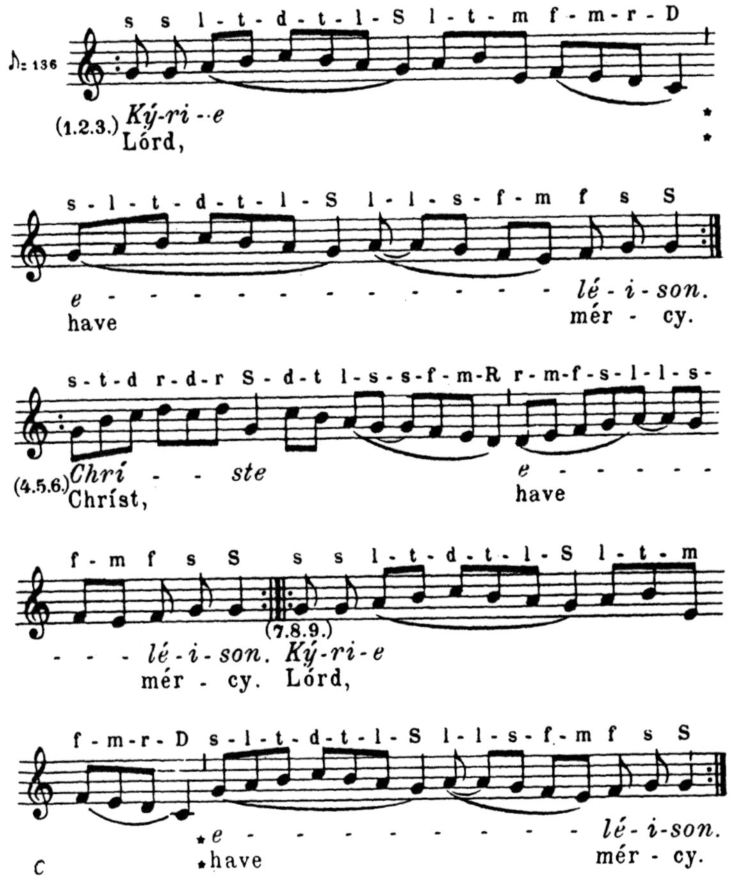
s s l - t - d - t - l - S l - t - m f - m - r - D
♪= 136
(1.2.3.) *Ký-ri - e*
Lórd,
s - l - t - d - t - l - S l - l - s - f - m f s S
e - - - - - - - - - - - - lé - i - son.
have mér - cy.
s - t - d r - d - r S - d - t l - s - s - f - m-R r - m-f - s - l - l - s -
(4.5.6.) *Chri - - ste e - - - - -*
Chríst, have
f - m f s S s s l - t - d - t - l - S l - t - m
- - - lé-i - son. Ký-ri - e
mér - cy. Lórd,
(7.8.9.)
f - m - r - D s - l - t - d - t - l - S l - l - s - f - m f s S
e - - - - - - - - - - lé- i-son.
have mér - cy.

C

Sanctus

Mode VIII

11th century

♪= 136
s-l d-t-d L-S r-m-r s-l d-t-d L-S s-l-m f-r-D
Hó - ly, *Hó - - ly, Hó - -
s-l-m f-s S s l-d-t d-l-s l-f S r m-r d-t-r
- - ly Lórd Gód of hósts. Héa-ven and
d-t d-l-s f-l d-s l-f S r d-t l-s f-s-l-l-m M
éarth are fúll of thy gló - ry.
s-l d-s l-f l l S l-s-f m-r-d D m-f-s l-s-
Gló - ry be to thée, O Lórd most
l-m f-s S r-m-r d-r r-m-r-r S s-l-t d-l-s-s
hígh. Bléss - ed is hé that
f-s-l d-s l-f S l t-d s f s-l D r-m d-t-d
cóm - - eth in the Náme of the Lórd. Ho - -
l-l S l-s-f m-r-d D m-f-s l-s l-m f-s S
- sán - na in the hígh - - - est.

Agnus Dei

Mode VIII 12th century

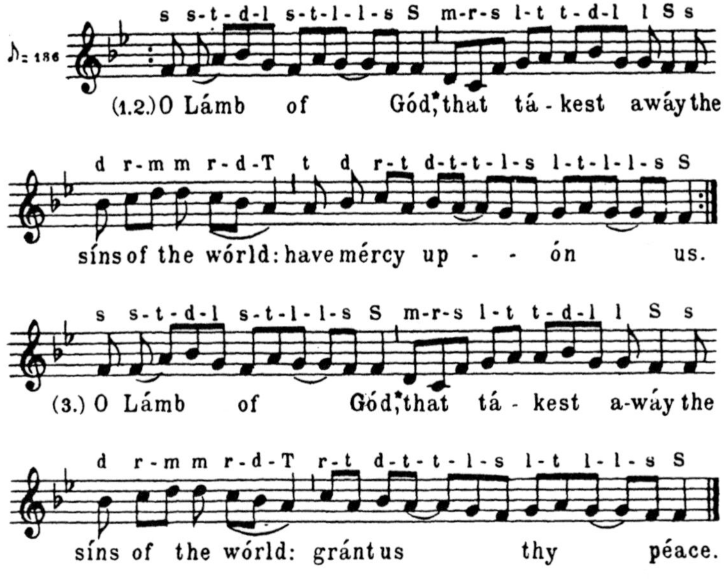
♪= 186
s s-t-d-l s-t-l-l-s S m-r-s l-t t-d-l l S s
(1.2.) O Lámb of Gód,* that tá - kest awáy the
d r-m m r-d-T t d r-t d-t-t-l-s l-t-l-l-s S
síns of the wórld: have mércy up - - ón us.
s s-t-d-l s-t-l-l-s S m-r-s l-t t-d-l l S s
(3.) O Lámb of Gód,* that tá - kest a-wáy the
d r-m m r-d-T r-t d-t-t-l-s l-t l-l-s S
síns of the wórld: gránt us thy péace.

Gloria in excelsis

Mode VIII 12th century

♪= 144
s f-m-r r m-f-s s-f l-s S s t d-r R
Gló-ry be to Gód on hígh, And in éarth péace,
t r-d-t-l-s l-t l-s S d-s l-s m-f-m-R
good-wíll to - wards men. We práise thee.

r m-f-s-s-f L-S s t d-r t-l-T r d-t l-s
We bléss thee. We wór-ship thee. We gló-ri-
l-t-l S d-l-s l-s m-f-m-R r-m-f-s-s-f L-S
-fy thee. We give thánks to thée
s t-d-r r-d-t-l-s l-t-l S d-l-s l-s m-f-m R m-f-S
for thy great gló - ry. O Lórd Gód,
s f l S s t-d-r r t-l-t r-d-t-l-s l-t l-s S
héa-ven-ly Kíng, Gód the Fá-ther Al - mígh - ty.
d-l-s l-s m-f-m-R r m-f-s s s s s S
O Lórd, the ón - ly be-gót-ten Són,
s-f l-s S s-t d-r t-l-T r-d-t-l-s l-t-l
Jé - su Chríst. O Lórd Gód, Lámb of
S d l-s l-s m-f-m-r R r m-f-s s s s
Gód, Són of the Fá - - ther. That tá - kest a-wáy

s s f l-s S s t-d r-t r-d-t-l-s l-t-l S S
the síns of the wórld, have mér - cy up - ón us.
r r m-f-s s s s s s f l-s S
[Thou that tá - kest a-wáy the síns of the wórld,
s t-d r-t r-d-t-l-s l-t-l S S d l-s l s
have mér - cy up - ón us.] Thou that tá-kest
m-f-m R r m-f-s f l-s S r d-t-l-s l-t-l S S
a - wáy the síns of the wórld, re-céive our práy-er.
d l-s l-s m-f-m R r r m-f-s s s s
Thou that sít - test at the ríght hánd of Gód
f l-s S s t-d r-t r-d-t-l-s l-t-l S S
the Fá-ther, have mér - - cy up - ón us.
d-l-s l-s m-f-m R m-f-s-f l-l S r m-f-s f l
For thou ón - ly art hó - ly. Thou ón - ly art

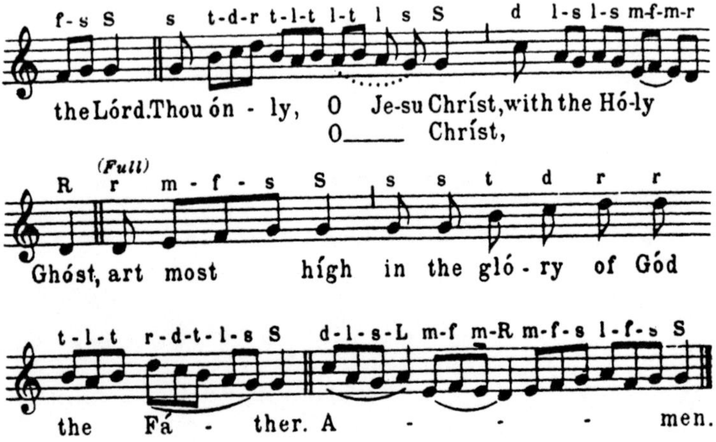
the Lórd. Thou ón - ly, O Je-su Chríst, with the Hó-ly
O Chríst,
(Full)
Ghóst, art most hígh in the gló - ry of Gód
the Fá - ther. A - - - men.

Ite, missa est

℟. Thánks
bé to Gód.

IV— ON DOUBLE FEASTS

Kyrie de Angelis

Mode V 16th century

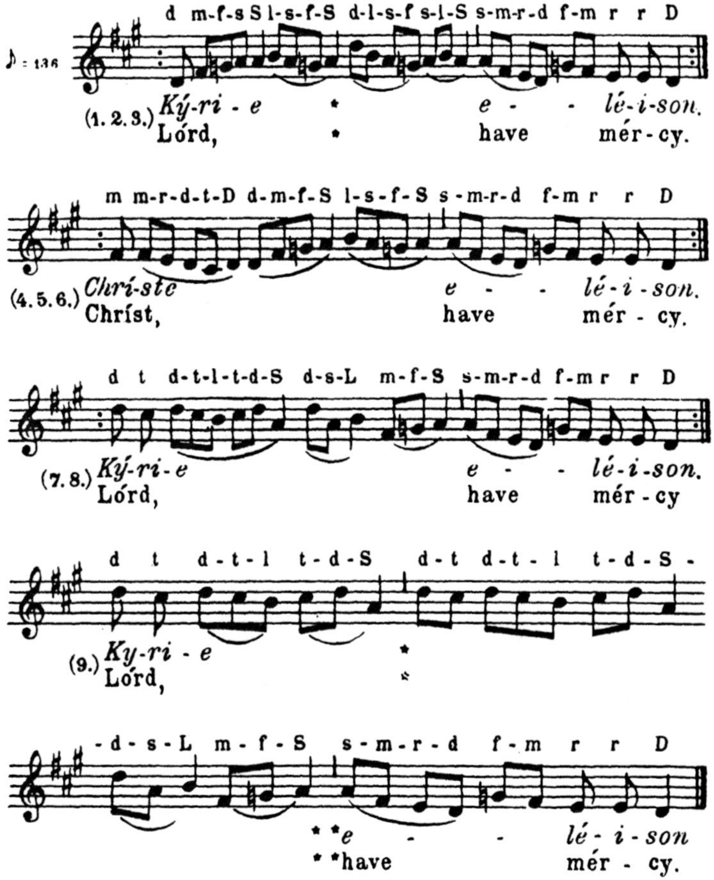
d m-f-s S l-s-f-S d-l-s-f s-l-S s-m-r-d f-m r r D
♪ = 136
(1. 2. 3.) Ký-ri - e * e - - lé-i-son.
Lórd, * have mér-cy.
m m-r-d-t-D d-m-f-S l-s-f-S s-m-r-d f-m r r D
(4. 5. 6.) Chrí-ste e - - lé-i-son.
Chríst, have mér - cy.
d t d-t-l-t-d-S d-s-L m-f-S s-m-r-d f-m r r D
(7. 8.) Ký-ri-e e - - lé-i-son.
Lórd, have mér - cy
d t d-t-l t-d-S d-t d-t-l t-d-S -
(9.) Ky-ri - e *
Lórd, *
-d-s-L m-f-S s-m-r-d f-m r r D
* *e - - lé - i - son
* *have mér - cy.

Sanctus

Mode V

16th century

s - m - d R - D d - m - s L - S s - m - d R - D
Hó - ly, *Hó - ly, Hó - ly
m - r - m s - l - s d - t L - S s f m s l - t
Lórd Gód of hósts. Héa-ven and éarth are
d s l L S d t l - s m - f S
fúll of thy gló - ry. Gló - ry be to thée,
m r - m d - r - d D d - m - s m - r s - l - s
O Lórd most high. Bléss - ed is hé
l - t d - t L - S m - r - m s l - s l - t - d
that cóm - eth in the Náme of
t L - S s - l d - t - l s m - r - m d r - d D
the Lórd. Ho - sán - na in the hígh - est.

Agnus Dei

Mode V

16th century

♪ = 138
s m-d r-f M d m s s l-s l d-t l-s
O Lámb of Gód,* that tákest a-wáy the síns of
m-f S s m-d r-m d r-d D m f-r m-f S
the wórld: have mér-cy up-ón us. O Lámb of God,*
s l s l d-t l s-f s-l l S s m-d
that tákest a-wáy the síns of the wórld: have mér-
r-m d r-d D d m-s m-d-r M d m s s
-cy up-ón us. O Lámb of God,* that tákest a-
l-s l d-t l-s m-f S s-m d-r-m f-m R-D
-wáy the síns of the wórld: gránt us thy péace.

Gloria in excelsis

Mode V

16th century

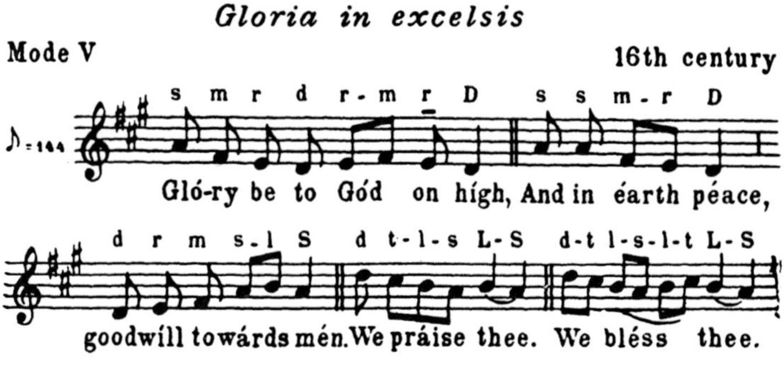
♪ = 144
s m r d r-m r D s s m-r D
Gló-ry be to Gód on hígh, And in éarth péace,
d r m s-l S d t-l-s L-S d-t l-s-l-t L-S
goodwill towárds mén. We práise thee. We bléss thee.

s m-r-d r-m D d r m s-l S s l-t d-t
We wór - ship thee. We gló-ri-fy thee. We give thánks
l-t L-S m r-d r-m R D s m r-D
to thée for thý great gló-ry. O Lórd Gód,
r m r D d r-m s-l-s l-t d-t l-s S
héa-ven-ly Kíng, Gód the Fá - ther Al - mígh-ty.
s M r d r m s l S l-t d-t L-S
O Lórd, the ón-ly-be-got-ten Són, Jé - su Chríst.
d t-l t-l-S l t L-S s s m-r-d r-m-r D
O Lórd Gód, Lámb of Gód, Són of the Fá - ther.
d r m s l s l-t d t L-S
That tá-kest a-wáy the síns of the wórld,
s m-r d r-m R D d d r m s l
have mér - cy up - ón us. [Thou that tá-kest a-wáy
s l-t d t L-S s m-r d r-m R D
the síns of the wórld, have mér - cy up - ón us.]

d t l s l-t l-s s m r d R-M s l-s
Thou that tákest a - wáy the síns of the wórld, re-ceíve
l-t-d-t L-S s m r d r m R D r
our práyer. Thou that síttest at the ríght hánd of
m s L S s l t d-t L S d t l s
Gód the Fáther, have mércy up - ón us. For thou ón-ly
l-t L S d t l-s l-t l-s S s-m r d r m s
art hó-ly. Thou ón-ly art the Lórd. Thou ón-ly, O Jé-su
O
(Full)
L-S l t d t L-S m-r-d r-m-r D d d
Chríst, with the Hó-ly Ghóst, art most hígh in the
r m s l s l-t d-t L-S s-m-r-d f-m-r R-D
gló-ry of Gód the Fá - ther. A - - men

Ite, missa est

d-m-f-s-S l-s-f S d-l-s-f s-l-S s-m r-d f-mr R-D
R: Thánks be to Gód.

V– ON DOUBLE FEASTS

O Pater excelse

Mode VIII

11th century

♪ = 132
s s s - f r - f s - l - S s - d - d - t - s
(1.2.3.) *Ký-ri-e*
Lórd,
l - s f s S l s - d - t - s - s - f - L
e - lé - i - son. (4.5.6.) *Chri-ste*
have mér - cy. Christ,
l - d - d - t l - s l - t - s - s - f - m f s S
e - - lé - i - son.
have mér - cy.
s - r d - r R f - r - r - d - M f - s - m - r
(7.8.9.) *Ký - ri - e*
Lórd,
f - m - R r - d - d - t l - s l - t - l l S
**e - - lé - i - son.*
*have mér - cy.

Sanctus

Mode VI 12th century

Hó - ly,*Hó - ly, Hó - - ly
Lórd Gód of hósts.
Héa-ven and éarth are fúll of thy gló - ry
Gló-ry be to thée, O Lórd most hígh.
Bléss-ed is hé that cóm - eth
in the náme of the Lórd. Ho - sán - - na
in the hígh - - est.

Agnus Dei

Mode VI | 15th century

Gloria in excelsis

Mode IV | Ambrosian

Glóry be to Gód on hígh, And in éarth péace,
good-wíll to-wárds mén. We práise thee. We bléss thee.
We wór - ship thee. We gló - ri - fy thee.
We give thánks to thée
for thý great gló - ry. O Lórd Gód,
héa - ven - ly Kíng, Gód the Fáther Al - mígh - ty.
O Lórd, the ónly - begótten Són, Jé - su

d - l - t - l - s - d - d - r - d - t - d l - t L - S l l S
Chríst. O Lórd Gód,
l l S l l l L S L-L
Lámb of Gód, Són of the Fá-ther. That tákest awáy the
t l s t - l - s - d - d - r - d - t - d l - s L - S
síns of the wórld,
l l l l L S L L
have mér - cy up - ón us. Thou that tákest awáy the
t l s t - l - s - d - d - r - d t - d l - t L - S l l l
síns of the wórld, have mér- cy
l L S L L t l s
up - ón us. Thou that tákest awáy the síns of the
t - l - s - d - d - r - d - t - d l - t L - S l l l S
wórld, recéive our práyer.
s l L-L l s
Thou that síttest at the ríght hánd of Gód the Fá - ther,

have mér-cy up - ón us. For thou ónly art hó - ly.
Thou ónly art the Lórd Thou ónly O (Jésu)
Chríst, with the Hó-ly Ghóst,
art most hígh in the gló - ry of Gód the
Fá-ther. A-men.

Ite, missa est

℟. Thánks be to Gód.

VI– ON FEASTS OF THE B. V. M.
and at Midnight on Christmas Eve

Alme Pater

Mode I — 11th century

♪ = 132
l - d - m - r d - t L t - l - s - l d l L
(1) *Ký - ri - - e* é - lé - i - son.*
Lórd, * have mér - cy.
m s - fe s - l t - l - s - l d l L
(2) *Ký - ri - e e - - lé - i - son.*
Lórd, have mér - cy.
l - d - m - r d - t L t - l - s - l d l L
(3) *Ký - - ri - e e - - lé - i - son.*
Lórd, have mér - cy.
m m - r m - r - d r m M
(4) *Chrí - ste e - - lé - i - son.*
Chríst, have mér - cy.
m - m - r d - t - L t - l - s - l d l L
(5) *Chrí - ste e - - lé - i - son*
Chríst, have mér - cy.
m m - r m - r - d r m M
(6) *Chrí - ste e - - le - i - son.*
Chríst, have mér - cy.

s l s - l - m - m - r m - r - d r m M
Ký - ri - e e - - lé - i - son.
(7) Lórd, have mér - cy.
m - m - r d - t L t - l - s - l d l L s l
Ký - ri - e e lé - i - son. (9) Ký - ri -
(8) Lórd, have mér - cy. Lórd,
s - l - m - m - r m - r - d - r M s - l s - l - m - m r
- e
m - r - d - r M m - r - d - t - L t - l - s - l d l L
e - - lé - i - son.
have mér - cy.

Sanctus

Mode V

11th century

♪ = 132
s - s - m - m - r D d - m - s - s - l S
Ho - - ly, Ho - - ly,
s - s m - m - r D m - s - s - l - s
Ho - - - ly Lord

s - l - t - d - l - s l - s S s f
God of hosts. Hea-ven
m - f - s s - f - r m - r - m D m - r r - s
and earth are full of thy
s - l - s S s - l - t - d l - s l - s m - f - s
glo - ry. Glo - ry be to
s - f - r m r - m d - r - d D
thee, O Lord most high.
d m - r r - s s s s - l S
Bless-ed is he that com - eth
d m - r m - s s - l s S s - l t - d - l - s
in the name of the Lord. Ho - -
l - s m - f - s - s - f - r m r - m d - r - d D
- san - na in the high - est.

Agnus Dei

Mode I 11th century

m - s f f - m d - r - m - M - R m s s - l
O Lámb of Gód, * that tá - kest
l l s - f s s - l s S - M s - f f m
a-wáy the síns of the wórld: have mér-cy
r - d m - f r R m s s - l L l
up - ón us. O Lámb of Gód,* that
l l l - s s s - t t t l - t L
tá-kest a - wáy the síns of the wórld:
l - s l l - t - l s - f M M m - s f f - m
have mér-cy up - ón us. O Lámb of
d - r - m - M - R m s s - l l l s - f s
Gód * that tá - kest a-wáy the síns
s - l s S - M s - f - m r - d m - f - r R
of the wórld: gránt us thy péace.

Gloria in excelsis

Mode I

12th century

m r-d r-m r t-d l-t d-t-L l l-m s-s r-m
♪ = 144
Gló-ry be to Gód on high. And in éarth péace,
m r d r-m M m-r d-t L d-l s-l L
goodwíll to-wárds mén. We práise thee. We bléss thee.
m r-d r-m M m s-l l s-fe M
We wór - ship thee. We gló - ri - fy thee.
m r-d r-m d-r-d L s-l d-t-l s-l L L
We give thánks to thée for thý great gló-ry.
m r-d R-M m r d R-L s l-d d-r d
O Lórd Gód, héa-ven-ly King, Gód the Fá - ther
d-t-l s-l L l m r m r d r d-t L
Al - mígh-ty. O Lórd, the ón-ly-be-gót-ten Són,

d - d - t s - l L m r - d R - M m r - d R - M
Jé - su Christ. O Lórd Gód, Lámb of Gód,
m r d r - m M l - m - r m - f m m m m
Són of the Fá - ther, That tá - kest a-wáy the
r d r - m M d - r m - r - d r r r - d L
síns of the wórld, have mér - cy up - ón us.
l - m - r m m - f m m m m r d r - m M
[Thou that tá - kest a-wáy the síns of the wórld,
d - r m - r - d r r r - d L l - m - r m m - f m m m
have mér - cy up - ón us.] Thou that tá - kest a-wáy
m r d r - m M d - r m - r - d r - d L
the síns of the wórld, re - ceíve our práyer.
s s s - l l l l d d t l
Thou that sít - test at the right hánd of Gód

t L S t - d - r d - t l d t - l L
the Fá-ther, have mér - cy up - ón us.
s s - l l - m r d r - m M l - m r d r
For thou ón - ly art hó - ly. Thou ón - ly art
r - m M l - m m r r - m r d - t L
the Lórd. Thou ón - ly O Jé - su Christ,
O Chríst,
(Full)
d - d - t l s s - l L l - m r - d R - M d d
with the Hó-ly Ghóst, art most hígh in the
r - m m m m - r - d r r - d L d - d - t s - l L
gló - ry of Gód the Fá - ther. A - - men.

Ite, missa est

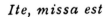

l - d - r - m - r - d T - L d - l s - l s - l d - r d T - L
R: Thánks be to Gód.

VII—ON SUNDAYS

Orbis factor

Mode I

10th century

♪ = 132
m - f m - r M - L d - r - m f - m - r d - t - l
(1.2.3.) *Ký - ri - e* * *e - - -*
Lórd, * have
s l L m - r L s - l - s m - r M d - r - m
-lé - i - son. Chrí - ste e -
mér - cy. (4.5.6.) Chríst, have
f - m - r d - t - l s l L m - f m - r M - L
- - - lé - i - son. Ký - ri - e
mér - cy. (7.8.) Lórd,
d - r - m f - m - r d - t - l s l L l - d - l s - l
e - - lé - i - son. Ký - ri -
have mér - cy. (9.) Lórd,
L - R - d - r - d - l - s - L d - r - m f - m - r d - t - l s l L
*-e * e - - lé - i - son.*
* have mér - cy.

Sanctus

Mode V

14th century

s-s-m-m-d-r-m-r D m-m-r D d-m-s-s d-t-l-t
Hó - - ly,* Hó - ly, Hó - -
L-S d-t-l-S m-d f-d-r-m R-D m m-r d
-ly Lórd Gód of hósts. Héa-ven and
r-m s l-t-l-L-S d t-l-s-m f-m-r-m R-D
éarth are fúll of thy gló - ry.
m s-l-s s s m d r-m r R-D d-t-l-t
Gló-ry be to thée, O Lórd most hígh. Bléss - -
s l-t T l-t d-t-l S d t-l-s-l-t L-S
-ed is hé that cóm - eth in the Náme
m-d f-m-r-m R-D d-r-m-d-r-m-f-m-r-M-d-m
of the Lórd. Ho - -
s-s-l S d t-l-s m-r-D-m-s-m-d-r-d D
-sán - na in the hígh - - est.

Agnus Dei

Mode V 13th century

O Lámb of God,* that tá - kest a - wáy
the síns of the wórld: have mér - cy
up - ón us. O Lámb of Gód,*
that tá - kest a - wáy the síns of the wórld:
have mér - cy up - ón us. O Lámb of
Gód,* that tá - kest a - wáy the síns
of the wórld: gránt us thy péace.

Gloria in excelsis

Mode II 10th century

Gló - ry be to Gód on hígh,
And in éarth péace, good - wíll to -
-wárds mén. We práise thee. We bléss thee.
We wór-ship thee. We gló-ri - fy thée.
We give thánks to thée for thý great
gló-ry. O Lórd Gód, héa-ven-ly Kíng,
Gód the Fá - ther Al - mígh - ty.

l - r d - t d - r d - t l t - d t l S
O Lórd, the ón - ly- be - gót-ten Són,
l - s t - d - t L l - r d - t d - r d - t - L t d T - L
Jé - su Chríst. O Lórd Gód, Lámb of Gód,
l - s t d - t L L t s - l l l l l - s
Són of the Fá-ther, That tá - kest a-wáy the
t d t - l - l S l l - s t d - t L L
síns of the wórld, have mér - cy up - ón us.
t t s - l l l l l - s t d t - l - l S
[Thou that tá - kest a-wáy the síns of the wórld,
l l - s t d - t L L t t s - l l l l
have mér- cy up - ón us.] Thou that tá - kest a-wáy
l - s t d t - l - l S l - s t d - t L
the síns of the wórld, re - céive our práyer.
l l - r d t d r d d - t l
Thou that sít-test at the ríght hánd of

t d T L l l - s t d - t L L
Gód the Fá-ther, have mér - cy up - ón us.
l - r d - t d - r d - t - l t d T L l - s t
For thou ón - ly art hó-ly, Thou ón -
d t l S l - s t d d t l S l l - s
-ly art the Lórd. Thou ón-ly, O Jé-su Christ, O Christ, with the
(Full)
t - d - t l L l - t s - l S s t r r r - m
Hó - ly Ghóst, árt most hígh in the gló-ry of
r - d - T t t - r - r - d - l - s - l - t - d T - L s - t - d - l S - L
Gód the Fá - - ther. A - men.

Ite, missa est

m - f - m - r - M - L d - r - m - f - m - r - d - t - l s - l L
Thánks be to Gód.
℟. A - - - men.

VIII– ON SEMI-DOUBLE FEASTS

Pater cuncta

Mode VIII | 12th century

s l t - s r - d t - l - S l - s l - t - l l S
♪ = 132
(1.2.3.) *Ký-ri-e* * *e - lé - i - son.*
Lórd, * have mér - cy.
s s - m s - f - m - R f m f S
(4.5.6.) *Chrí-ste e - le - i - son.*
Chríst, have mér - cy.
s l t - s r - d t - l - S l - s l - t - l l S
(7.8.) *Ký-ri - e e - lé - i - son.*
Lórd, have mér - cy.
s l t - s r - d t - l - S - s - m s - f - m - R f m f S
(9) *Ký-ri - e* * *e - lé - i - son.*
Lórd, *have mér - cy.

Sanctus

Mode VIII 13th century

♪ = 132
s - l S m - f R m s s - l - t d - l - s f - s S
Hó - ly,* Hó - ly, Hó-ly Lórd Gód of hósts.
s t d r r - d r - t d l - l S S
Héa-ven and éarth are fúll of thy gló-ry.
l l s - m s l - t t - l - s l s S
Gló-ry be to thée, O Lórd most hígh.
s s s l s f - m R m - s m r
Bléss-ed is hé that cóm - eth in the náme
m s S s l - t d - l - s - f l l - t - l S S
of the Lórd. Ho-sán-na in the hígh-est.

Agnus Dei

Mode I 14th century

♪ = 132
l-t-d-l l-s s-l L t r m r d-t t-d-r
O Lámb of Gód,* that tá-kest a-wáy the
r-d-t l-s l-t T r-m r l d-t-l s-l L
síns of the wórld: have mér-cy up - ón us.
l-t r-m m-f M r m r d t-l T d
O Lámb of Gód,* that tá-kest a - wáy the
r l d-t-l S t-r-m r d t-l s-l L
síns of the wórld: have mér-cy up - ón us.
l t r-d-t r M m-r s l s fe m
O Lámb of Gód,* that tá-kest a-wáy the
r-m-d t l-t t-l-S t-r-m d-t-l s-l L
síns of the wórld: gránt us thy péace.
E

Gloria in excelsis

Mode IV 12th century

r-l s-f-m r m f-s l-s-f-m M m f s-l s
♪ = 144
Gló-ry be to God on hígh. And in éarth péace,
s l s m-f-s M r f-m R m-f s-f-m M
good-wíll to-wárds mén. We práise thee. We bléss thee.
f s f-m M s l s f-m M m s l
We wór-ship thee. We gló-ri-fy thee. We give thánks
t-d l s f s-l S M r m F
to thee for thý gréat gló-ry. O Lórd Gód,
s s f S l l s f l s-f-m M
héa-ven-ly Kíng, Gód the Fá-ther Al-mígh - ty.
m f m r m f s f s l-s f-m M
O Lórd, the ón-ly be-gót-ten Són, Jé - su Chríst.

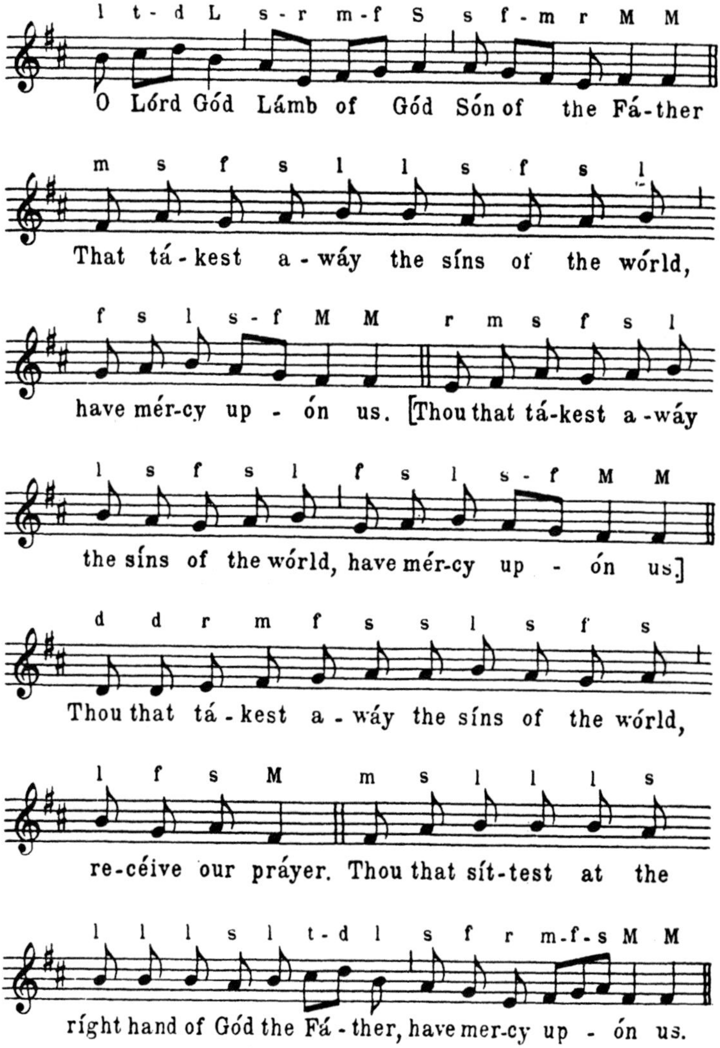
l t-d L s-r m-f S s f-m r M M
O Lórd Gód Lámb of Gód Són of the Fá-ther
m s f s l l s f s l
That tá-kest a-wáy the síns of the wórld,
f s l s-f M M r m s f s l
have mér-cy up-ón us. [Thou that tá-kest a-wáy
l s f s l f s l s-f M M
the síns of the wórld, have mér-cy up-ón us.]
d d r m f s s l s f s
Thou that tá-kest a-wáy the síns of the wórld,
l f s M m s l l l s
re-céive our práyer. Thou that sít-test at the
l l l s l t-d l s f r m-f-s M M
ríght hand of Gód the Fá-ther, have mer-cy up-ón us.

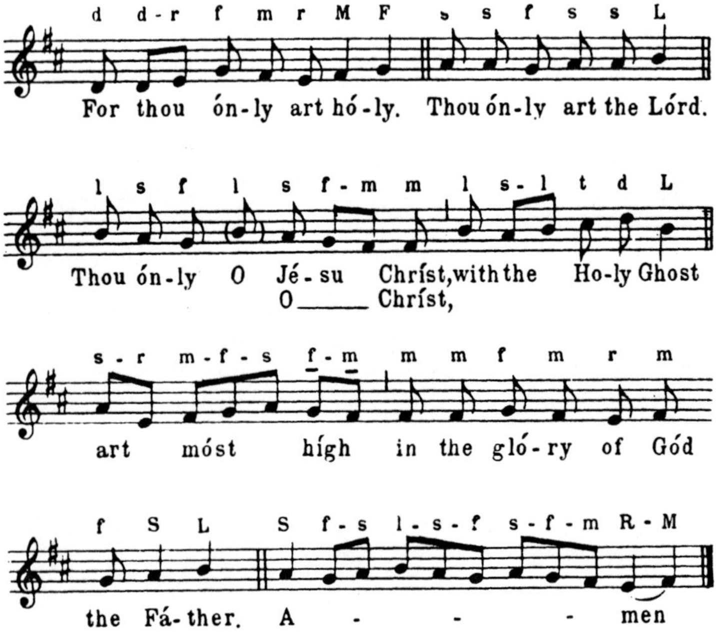
d d - r f m r M F s s f s s L
For thou ón-ly art hó-ly. Thou ón-ly art the Lórd.
l s f l s f - m m l s - l t d L
Thou ón-ly O Jé-su Chríst, with the Ho-ly Ghost
O______ Chríst,
s - r m - f - s f - m m m f m r m
art móst hígh in the gló-ry of Gód
f S L S f - s l - s - f s - f - m R - M
the Fá-ther. A - - - men

Ite, missa est

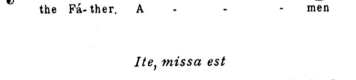

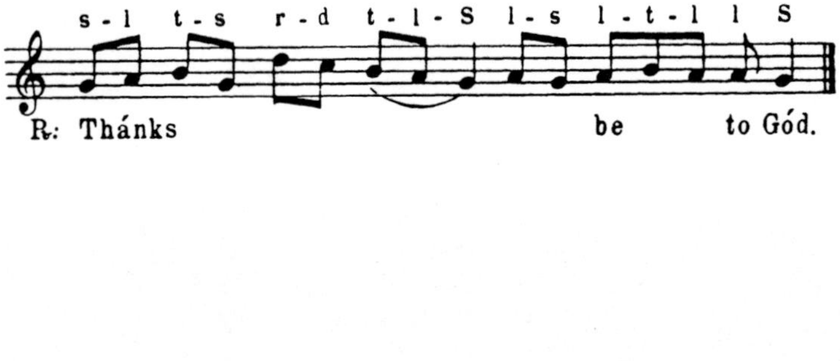
s - l t - s r - d t - l - S l - s l - t - l l S
℟: Thánks be to Gód.

IX – WITHIN OCTAVES
which are not of the B. V. M.

Splendor aeterne

Mode I

11th century

r r r-d-d-l-d-R r-s-l f-f-m r-d m-f r R
♪ = 132
(1.2.3.) Ký-ri-e *e - - lé - i-son.
Lórd, *have mér - cy.
l s-l-s-F s-m-f-M-R d-m-s-s-m f-m-r-m-r-r
(4.5.6.) Chrí-ste e - -
Chríste, have
d-r-m m R l l l-s d-r-d-t-l D-L t-l-s-m
-lé - i-son. (7.8.) Ký-ri-e e -
mér - cy. Lórd, have
s-l-t t L l l l-s d-r-d-t-l D-L t-l-s-m
-lé - i-son. (9.) Ký-ri-e
mér - cy. Lórd,
s-l T-L d-r-d-t-l D-L t-l-s-m S-L l-t-l-s-l-s
M-R d-m-s-s-m f-m-r-m-r-r d-r-m m R
** e - - lé - i-son.
** have mér - cy.

Sanctus

Mode I — 12th century

♪ = 132
l - t - d - t - s d - d T - L d - r - m - r - d r - r D - T
Hó - - ly, *Hó - - ly,
l - t - d - t - s d - d T - L m - r - d t - l t - r - t d - l t - s - l L
Hó - - ly Lórd Gód of hósts.
m r m l - s - fe s - l M m - f - m - r d - t - L
Héa-ven and éarth are fúll
s t - r m - r - d T - L l - d - l t - s t s L r - m
of thy gló - ry. Gló - ry be to thée, O
l - t d - t - s - d - d d T - L l - s - fe s - l m m - fe s - fe - r s - s
Lórd most hígh. Bléss - ed is
Fe - M m - f - m - r d - t L s t - r m - r - d t l L
hé that cóm-eth in the náme of the Lórd.
t - r - t d - l t - s L s - t r - m l - t - d - t - s d - d T - L
Ho - - sán-na in the hígh - - est.

Agnus Dei

Mode IV | 12th century

D-r-m-f f-m r-d-r m-f-s F-M s s-l d-l s
♪ = 132
(1.2.3.) O Lámb of Gód, *that tá - kest

l f-f-m s-s-f m-f-m-r r-d r-m-f-s R-M
a-wáy the síns of the wórld:

first and second verses:

s-l l-d-l-s-l-s f-m r m-f-m-r s-l-s F-M
have mér - - cy up-ón us.

third verse:

s-l l-d-l-s-l-s f-m m-f-m-r s-l-s F-M
gránt us thy péace.

¶ *Any of the foregoing settings of* Gloria in excelsis *may be sung.*

Ite, missa est

s-l-s-l-s-s r-s f-s-f-m-R r-m f-s-l-l-s f-s S
℟. Thánks be to Gód.

x—On Simple Feasts

Dominator Deus

Mode IV

11th century

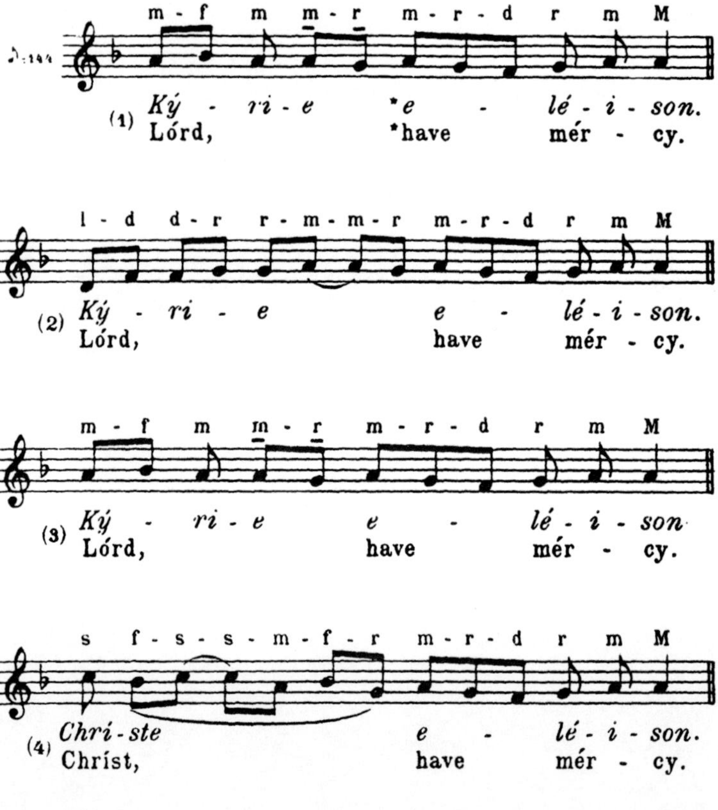
m - f m m - r m - r - d r m M
(1) *Ký - ri - e *e - lé - i - son.*
Lórd, *have mér - cy.
l - d d - r r - m - m - r m - r - d r m M
(2) *Ký - ri - e e - lé - i - son.*
Lórd, have mér - cy.
m - f m m - r m - r - d r m M
(3) *Ký - ri - e e - lé - i - son*
Lórd, have mér - cy.
s f - s - s - m - f - r m - r - d r m M
(4) *Chri - ste e - lé - i - son.*
Christ, have mér - cy.

r - m f - m M r - m - d r m M
(5) *Chrí - - ste e - lé - i - son.*
Chríst, have mér - cy.
s f - s - s - m - f - r m - r - d r m M
(6) *Chrí-ste e - lé - i - son.*
Chríst, have mér - cy.
s s - l l - s - f - s - s - m - f - r m - r - d r m M
(7) *Ky - ri - e e - lé - i - son.*
Lórd, have mér - cy.
d r - m m - r f - m - r - d - r - f r m M
(8) *Ký - ri - e e - - - le - i - son.*
Lórd, have mér - cy.
s f - m r - d S - f - s - l - s - f s s M
(9) *Ký - ri - e *e - - - lé - i - son.*
Lórd, *have mér - cy.

Sanctus

Mode IV

♪ = 132
m - m - s M f - f - f R - D r - f - r M
Hó - ly, *Hó - ly, Hó - ly,
s - f s f - m M s f r - d r - f r - m M
Lórd Gód of hósts. Héa-ven and éarth are fúll
s f - s f - m M s s - l l s f s
of thy gló - ry. Gló - ry be to thée, O
s - s m M s m f r - d r
Lórd most hígh. Bléss - ed is hé that
r - f - r M s f s s f - m M
cóm - eth in the Náme of the Lórd.
s s - l l s f S M
Ho - sán - na in the hígh - est.

Agnus Dei

Mode IV 12th century

m r - d r - m M m s l l l s - f
O Lámb of Gód, *that tá-kest a-wáy the
s s f - m M m - r f r r - m M M
síns of the wórld: have mér - cy up - ón us.
s s s L s - f s l l l s - f
O Lámb of Gód, *that tá-kest a - wáy the
s s f - m M f - m f - s f - f - m r - d r - m M
síns of the wórld: have mér - cy up - ón us.
m r - d r - m M m s l l l
O Lámb of Gód, *that tá - kest a - wáy
s - f s s f - m M m - r f r - m M
the síns of the wórld: gránt us thy péace.

Gloria in excelsis

Mode IV | 10th century

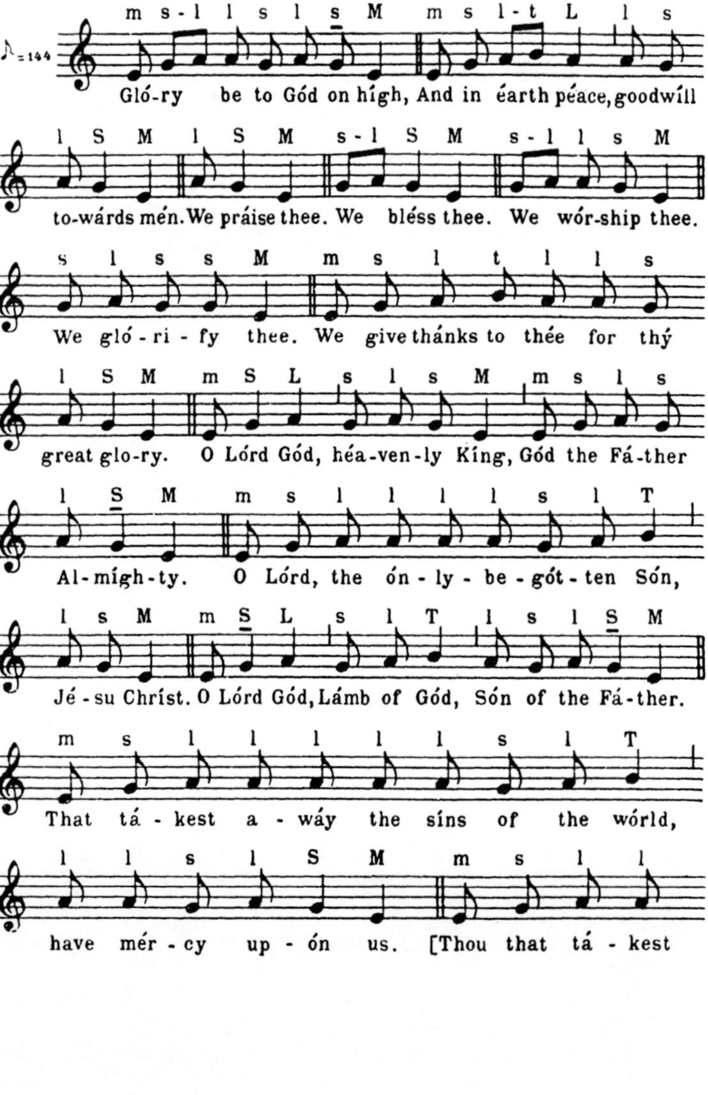
♪ = 144
m s - l l s l s M m s l - t L l s
Gló-ry be to Gód on hígh, And in éarth péace, goodwíll
l S M l S M s - l S M s - l l s M
to-wárds mén. We práise thee. We bléss thee. We wór-ship thee.
s l s s M m s l t l l s
We gló - ri - fy thee. We give thánks to thée for thý
l S M m S L s l s M m s l s
great glo-ry. O Lórd Gód, héa-ven-ly Kíng, Gód the Fá-ther
l S M m s l l l l s l T
Al-mígh-ty. O Lórd, the ón - ly - be - gót - ten Són,
l s M m S L s l T l s l S M
Jé - su Chríst. O Lórd Gód, Lámb of Gód, Són of the Fá-ther.
m s l l l l l s l T
That tá - kest a - wáy the síns of the wórld,
l l s l S M m s l l
have mér - cy up - ón us. [Thou that tá - kest

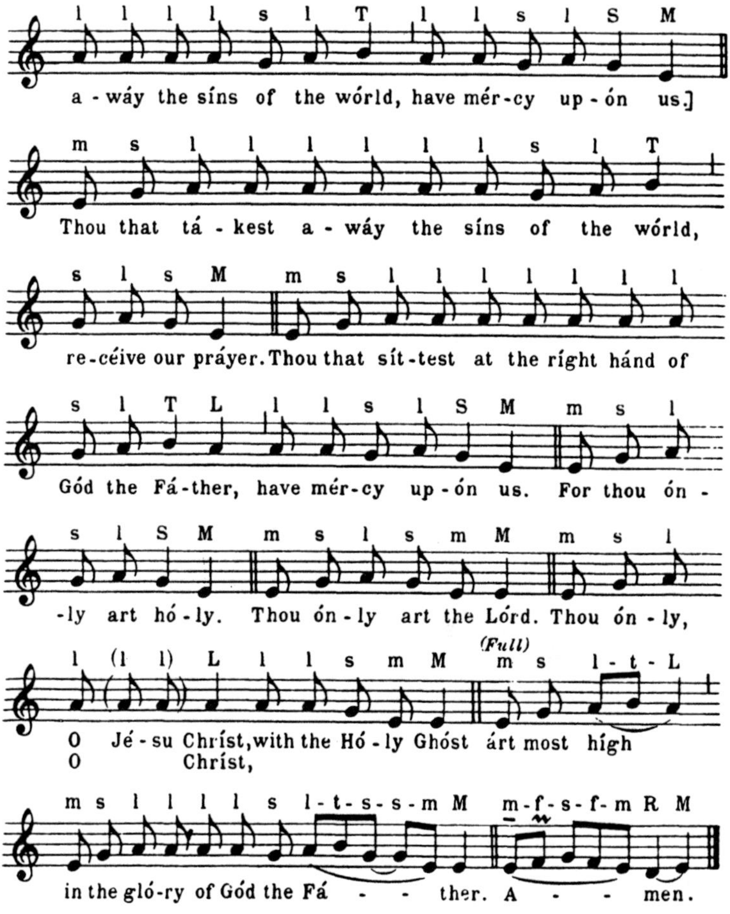
a - wáy the síns of the wórld, have mér-cy up - ón us.]
Thou that tá - kest a - wáy the síns of the wórld,
re-céive our práyer. Thou that sít-test at the ríght hánd of
Gód the Fá-ther, have mér-cy up - ón us. For thou ón -
-ly art hó - ly. Thou ón - ly art the Lórd. Thou ón - ly,
(Full)
O Jé - su Chríst, with the Hó - ly Ghóst árt most hígh
O Chríst,
in the gló-ry of Gód the Fá - - ther. A - - men.

Ite, missa est

℟ Thánks be to Gód.

XI — On Ferias

Kyrie eleison

11th century

Sanctus

13th century

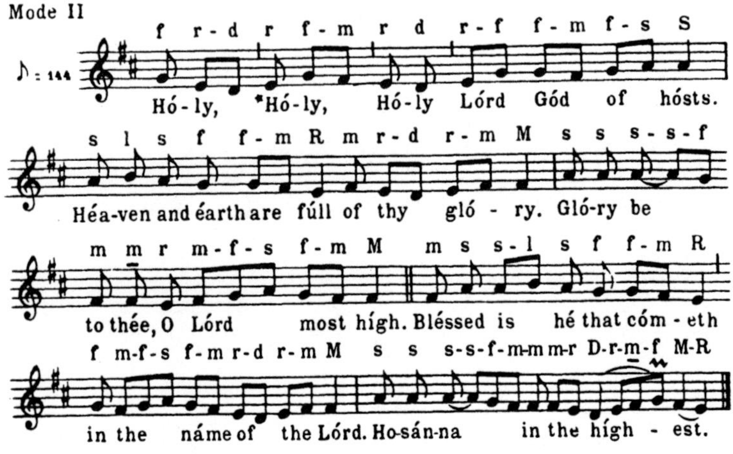

¶ *The setting of* Agnus Dei *given on page* 49 *should be used.*

Benedicamus Domino:

l s-l s s-f-M
℟. Thánks be to God.

XII-ON SUNDAYS IN ADVENT AND LENT

Kyrie eleison

Mode I 15th century

d r-f m-r-d r-f-r-M m-f s-f-m-r d-r-m f m R
♪= 132
(1.2.3.) Kýri - e *e - - lé-i-son.
Lórd, *have mér - cy.
f-s-l-s-f M-R m-f s-f-m-r d-r-m f m R
(4.5.6.) Chrí - ste e - - lé - i - son.
Chríst, have mér - cy.
l s-l L d r-d-t-L d-t-l s-l-t d t L
(7.8.) Ký-ri - e e - - lé- i - son.
Lórd, have mér - cy.
l s-l L d-r-d-t-L d-t-l-s-t-d-L
(9.) Ký-ri - e
Lórd,
l-s L d-r-d-t-L d-t-l-s-t-d L
l-s l-ta-l-S m-f-m-r d-r-m f m R
e - - - lé - i - son.
have mér - cy

Sanctus

Mode I — 11th century

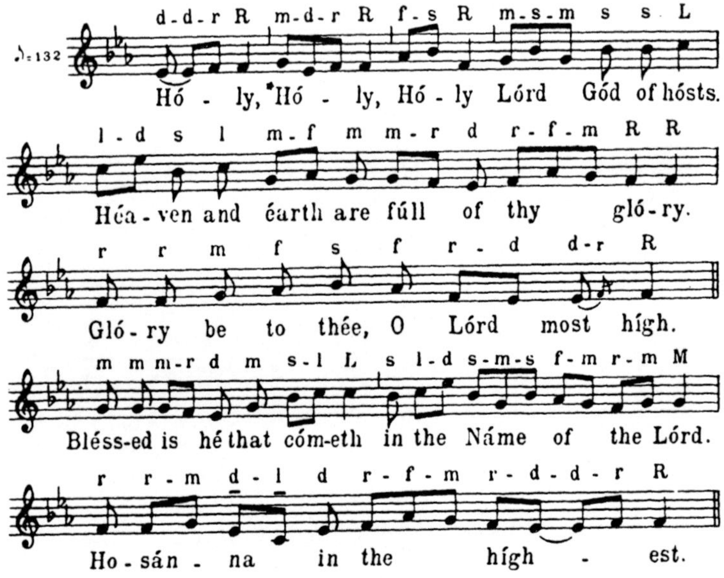
♪=132
Hó - ly, *Hó - ly, Hó - ly Lórd Gód of hósts.
Héa - ven and éarth are fúll of thy gló - ry.
Gló - ry be to thée, O Lórd most hígh.
Bléss-ed is hé that cóm-eth in the Náme of the Lórd.
Ho - sán - na in the hígh - est.

Agnus Dei

Mode VI

♪=132
O Lámb of Gód,* that tá-kest a-wáy the síns of the wórld:
first and second verses:
have mér- cy up - ón us.
third verse:
gránt us thy péace.

¶ *Gloria in Excelsis Deo* is not sung.

Benedicamus Domino

℟. Thánks be to Gód.

XIII — On Sundays in Advent and Lent

Kyrie eleison

Mode VI

14th century

♪ = 132
d r - d - r M s - f - m - r - m - d - t r - m - r r D
(1.2.3.) Ký-ri - e * e - - lé - i-son.
Lórd, * have mér - cy
s S m - f - S s - f - m - r - m - d - t r - m - r r D
(4.5.6.) Chrí-ste e - - lé - i-son.
Chríst, have mér - cy
d m - s s - s - l - f - S s - f - m - r - m - d - t r - m - r r D
(7.8.) Ký-ri - e e - - lé - i-son.
Lórd, have mér - cy
d m - s s - s - l - f - S d - m - s - s - s - l - f S
(9) Ký-ri - e *
Lórd, *
s - f - m - r - m - d - t r - m - r r D
e - - lé - i - son.
have mér - cy

¶ *The setting of the* Sanctus *on page 76 may be sung.*
The setting of Agnus Dei *on page 76 may be sung.*
Gloria in excelsis *is not sung.*

Benedicamus Domino

d r - d - r M s - f - m - r - m - d - t r - m - r r D
℟. Thánks be to Gód.

F

XIV— On Ferias in Advent and Lent and on Vigils, Ember Days and Rogation Days

Kyrie eleison

Mode IV 11th century

♪ = 132
d - d - t l - t l s l t T r r - m r - d
(1.2.3.) *Ký - ri - e* e - lé - i - son.* (4.5.6.) *Chrí - ste e -*
Lórd, *have mér - cy. Chríst, have

r r T d - d - t l - t l s l t T
- lé - i - son. (7.8.) *Ký - ri - e e - lé - i - son.*
mér - cy. Lórd, have mér - cy.

t - d - r l - t l - s r - d r - m - r - d r r T
(9) *Ký - ri - e * e - - lé - i - son.*
Lórd, * have mér - cy.

¶ *The setting of the* Sanctus *on page 125 should be sung*

Agnus Dei

12th century

♪ = 132
s s s - l L l l l l l s l f s L
(1.2.3.) O Lámb of Gód,* that tá-kest a-wáy the síns of the wórld,

l t s s l - s S
have mér-cy up-ón us.

t s l - s S
gránt us thy péace.

Benedicamus Domino:

l s - l s s - f - M
℟. Thánks be to Gód.

XV–MISSA SIMPLICIOR

(JOHN MERBECKE)

Kyrie eleison

Mode VI

♪ = 144
d r m r - m R D f m (m)
(1.2.3.) *Ký - ri - e e - léi-son* (4.5.6.) *Chrí - ste*
Lórd, have mér-cy up - ón us. Chríst, have mér -
r - m R D s f m r - m R D
e - léi - son. (7.8.9.) *Ký - ri - e e - léi - son.*
-cy up - ón us. Lórd, have mér-cy up - ón us.

Sanctus

Mode II

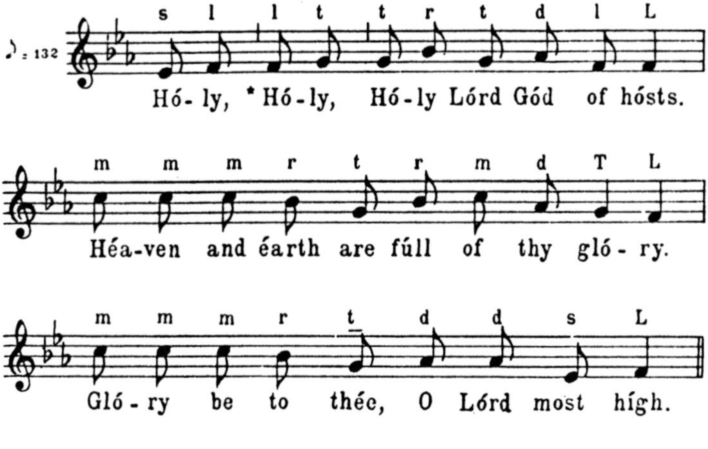
♪ = 132
s l l t t r t d l L
Hó - ly, * Hó - ly, Hó - ly Lórd Gód of hósts.
m m m r t r m d T L
Héa-ven and éarth are fúll of thy gló - ry.
m m m r t d d s L
Gló - ry be to thée, O Lórd most hígh.

Bléss - ed· is hé that cóm - eth in the
Náme of the Lórd Ho - sán - na in the hígh - est.

Agnus Dei

Mode I

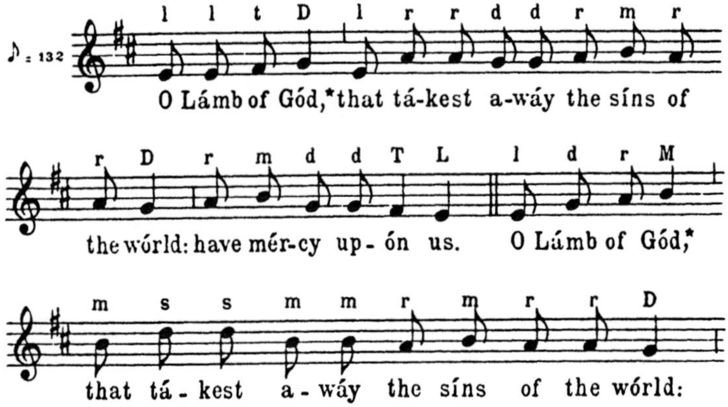
O Lámb of Gód,* that tá-kest a-wáy the síns of
the wórld: have mér-cy up - ón us. O Lámb of Gód,*
that tá - kest a - wáy the síns of the wórld:
have mér-cy up-ón us. O Lámb of Gód,* that tá -
- kest a-wáy the síns of the wórld: gránt us thy péace.

Gloria in excelsis

Mode IV

16th century

♪ = 144
d r f f m f S m f m r
Gló-ry be to Gód on hígh, and in éarth péace,
r s s s L s L L t D L
good-wíll to-wárds mén. We práise thee. We bléss thee.
l l l S m f f f M d r m
We wór-ship thee. We gló-ri-fy thee. We give thánks
m m s s m F M d r M f f
to thée for thý great gló-ry. O Lórd Gód, héa-ven-
f M s s l s l D S m f m
-ly Kíng, Gód the Fá-ther Al-mígh-ty. O Lórd, the
s s s f s L f f M d r F
ón-ly-be-gót-ten Són, Jé-su Chríst. O Lórd Gód,
m f S s f s L S m f f
Lámb of Gód, Són of the Fá-ther. That tá-kest
f m r m d r M f r d r M M
a-wáy the síns of the wórld, have mér-cy up-ón us.

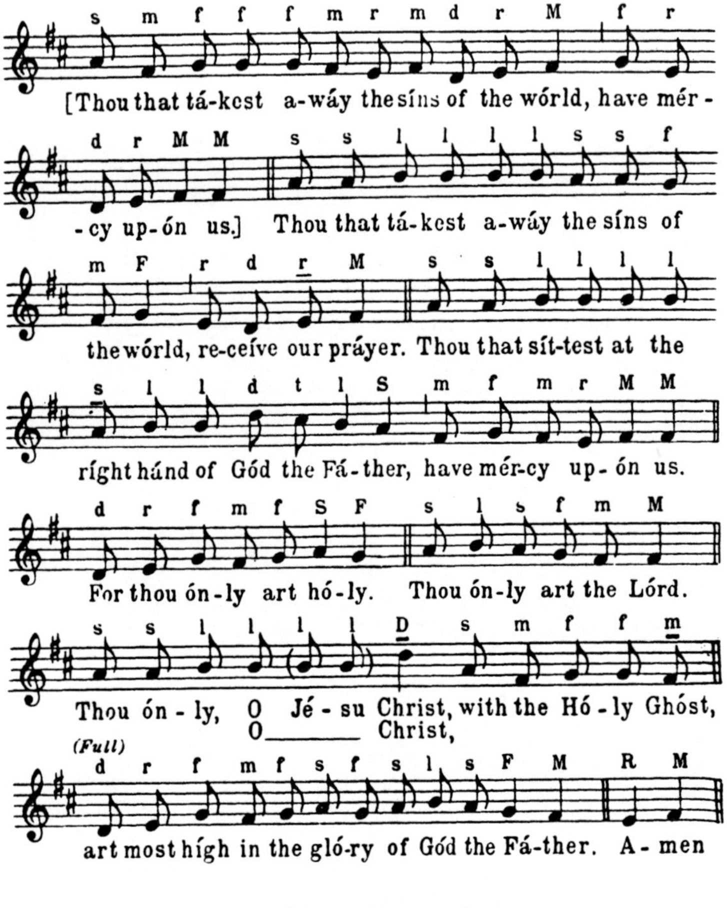
[Thou that tá-kest a-wáy the síns of the wórld, have mér-
-cy up-ón us.] Thou that tá-kest a-wáy the síns of
the wórld, re-ceíve our práyer. Thou that sít-test at the
ríght hánd of Gód the Fá-ther, have mér-cy up-ón us.
For thou ón-ly art hó-ly. Thou ón-ly art the Lórd.
Thou ón-ly, O Jé-su Christ, with the Hó-ly Ghóst,
O Christ,
(Full)
art most hígh in the gló-ry of Gód the Fá-ther. A-men

Ite, missa est

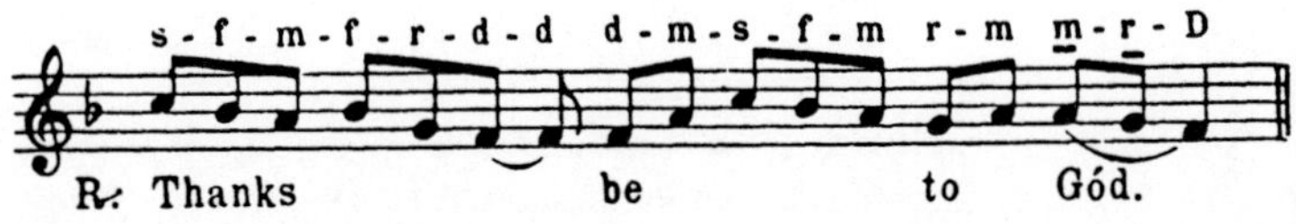
℟. Thanks be to Gód.

CREDO— I
(Authentic Tone)

Mode IV

11th century

♪ = 144
r t d l R M m - f m r d r r
I be-líeve in one God, the Fáther Almígh-ty,
t d r r d m R t d r m
Má-ker of héa - ven and earth, and of áll things
r d t l m - f m m r - d R t d r - d t - d - T
ví-si - ble, and in-ví - si - ble. And in óne Lórd
l t r - m m - f m m m r d m r - d R
Jé-sus Chríst, the ón- ly - be-gót-ten Són of Gód.
t - d r t l t R M m - f m r - d R
Be - gót-ten of his Fá-ther be - fóre all wórlds.
d m R r d t - d - T t r m m
Gód of Gód, Líght of Líght, Vé - ry Gód of
r d R t - d r r m - r T d l t d
Vé-ry Gód, Be - gót - ten, not máde, Bé-ing of óne

r t l t R M m-f m d m r-d R
súbstance with the Fá-ther: By whóm áll things were máde.
t d r-d t l t d r R R
Who for ús men, and for our sal-va-tion,
r d m R l t d r t d l t r
came dówn from héaven.*And was in-cár-nate by the Hó-ly
M m-f m r d R R d m r-d R
Ghóst of the Vír-gin Má-ry: And was máde mán.
t d r t d t l t r M
And was crú-ci-fi-ed ál-so for ús:

*The following phrase may be sung in harmony, if desired:

And was in-cár-nate by the Hó-ly Ghóst of the Vír-gin Má-ry: And was máde mán.

m - f m m r d R R m m - f m m r
un - der Pón-ti-us Pí-late he súf - fer-ed, and
d m r - d R t d r - t d l t r M
was bú-ri - ed. And the thírd dáy he róse a-gáin,
m - f m m r d R R t d r t
ac - córd-ing to the Scríp-tures. And as-cénd-ed
l t R M m - f m m m m m m r
in-to héa-ven: And sít-teth on the ríght hand of
d R R t-d r r r r r m r-d t-d - T
the Fá-ther. And he shall cóme a-gáin with gló-ry,
r - m m - f m d m r d R t - d r r
to júdge both the quíck and the déad: Whose kíng-dom
r d m R l t d r r r r r
shall háve no énd. And I be-líeve in the Hó - ly
M r - d T - L m - f m r d R t d r r
Ghóst, the Lórd, and Gív-er of life: Who pro-céed-eth

r r r r d m R l t d r m
from the Fá-ther and the Són. Who with the Fá-ther
r d T t d t l t r M
and the Són to - géth - er is wór-ship - ped
m - f m r - d R R t - d r d m R R
and glǿ-ri - fi - ed: Who spáke by the Pro-phets.
t - d r r D r - m r r r d t - l
And I be-líeve one Hó - ly, Cá - tho - lick
m - f m d m r - d R t d r d
and A - pos - tó - lick Church. I ac-knów-ledge
m r t t d r m d m R
one Báp - tism for the re - mís - sion of sins.
t d r t d l t r m d m R
And I lóok for the ré - sur - réc - tion of the déad,
t d r-d t l l-m-f m M m-r-d r-m-r-d-t L-T
And the lífe of the wórld to come. A - - men.

CREDO– II

(An English form of the Authentic Tone)

Mode IV

11th century

♪ = 144
r t d l R M m-m-f m r d r r
I be-líeve in óne Gód, the Fá-ther Al-mígh-ty,
t d r r d m R t d r r
Má-ker of héa-ven and éarth, and of áll thíngs
r d t-l l-m-m-f m m r-d R t d r t
ví-si-ble, and in-ví-si-ble. And in óne Lórd
l t r-m m-m-f m m m r d m r-d R
Jé-sus Chríst, the ón-ly-be-gótten Són of Gód.
t-d r t l t R M m-m-f m r-d R
Be-gót-ten of his Fá-ther be-fóre all wórlds.
d m R d m r-t l t r m d m R
Gód of Gód, Líght of Líght, Vé-ry Gód of vé-ry Gód,

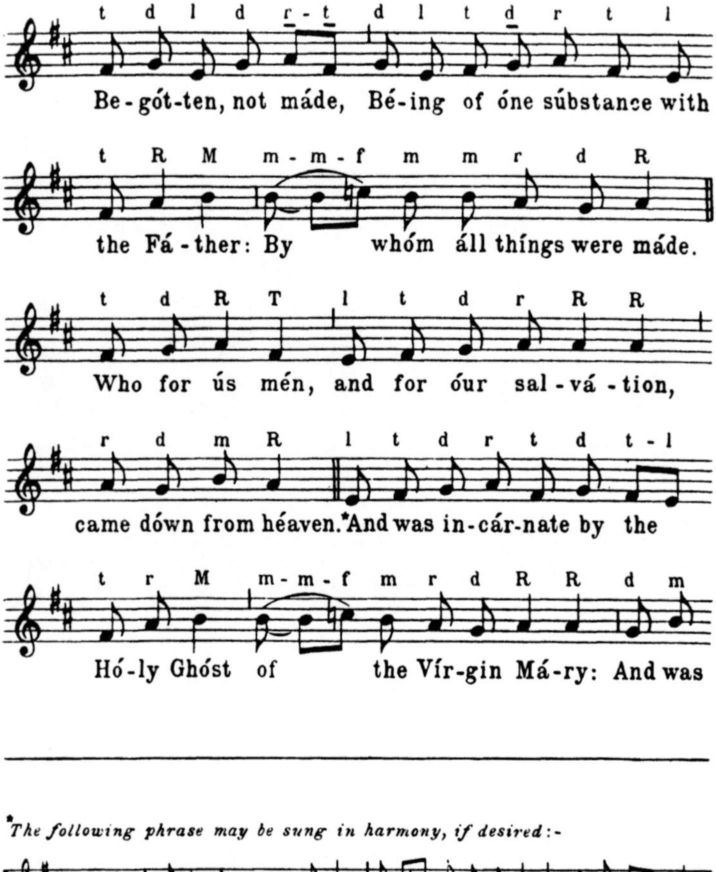
t d l d r - t d l t d r t l
Be-gót-ten, not máde, Bé-ing of óne súbstance with
t R M m - m - f m m r d R
the Fá-ther: By whóm áll thíngs were máde.
t d R T l t d r R R
Who for ús mén, and for óur sal-vá-tion,
r d m R l t d r t d t - l
came dówn from héaven.*And was in-cár-nate by the
t r M m - m - f m r d R R d m
Hó-ly Ghóst of the Vír-gin Má-ry: And was

**The following phrase may be sung in harmony, if desired:-*

And was in-cárnate by the Hó-ly Ghóst of the Vír-gin Má-ry: And was máde mán.

r - d R t d r t d t l t r M
máde mán. And was crú-ci-fi-ed ál-so for ús:
m-m-f m m r d R T m m m m r
un - der Pón-ti-us Pí-late he súf-fer-ed, and
d m r-d R t d r t l t r M
was bú-ri - ed. And the thírd dáy he róse a-gáin,
m-m-f m m r d R R t d r t
ac - córding to the Scríptures. And as-cénd-ed
l t R M m-m-f m m m m m m r
in-to héa-ven: And sít-teth on the ríght hánd of
d R R t-d r r r t l t R M
the Fá-ther. And hé shall cóme a-gáin with gló-ry,
m-m-f m m m m r d R t-d r r
to júdge both the quíck and the déad: Whose kíngdom
r d m R l t d r r r r r R
shall háve no énd. And I be-líeve in the Hó-ly Ghóst,

d t - l l - m - m - f m r d R t d r r
the Lórd, and Gív-er of lífe: Who procéedeth
r r r r d m R l t d r r r r
from the Fáther and the Són. Who with the Fáther and the
d t d t l t r M m-m-f m r-d R R
Són to-gé-ther is wór-shipped and__gló-ri - fi - ed:
t - d r d m R R t - d r r d
Who spáke by the Próphets. And I be-líeve
r-m r r r d t - l l-m-m-f m d m r-d R
one Hóly, Cátholick and A-pos-tó-lick Church.
t d r d r-m d t t d r r d m R
I ac-knówledge one Báptism for the remíssion of síns.
t d r t d l t r m d m R t d
And I loók for the re-sur-réc-tion of the déad, And the
r d t-l l-m-m-f m M m-r-d-r-r-m-r-d l-L-T
lífe of the wórld to cóme. A - - men.

CREDO – III
(de Angelis)

Mode V | 15th century

♪ = 132
s m d f m-r-d D m s m d r d
I belíeve in óne Gód, the Fáther Almíghty,
d m f s s l S s s l d t-s-l
Má-ker of héa-ven and eárth, and of áll things ví -
l S d f m-d-r r D s m D r-m
-si-ble, and in-ví - si-ble. And in óne Lórd
f r D m m m m f r s l S
Jé-sus Chríst, the ón-ly be-gót-ten Són of Gód.
m m r f f m-d-r D s m-d r D
Be-gót-ten of his Fá - ther be-fóre all wórlds.
s s m-d r m r-d s l s d t-s l S
Gód of Gód, Líght of Líght, Vé-ry Gód of vé - ry Gód.

m r f m-d-r D d d m s s s
Be-gót-ten, not máde, Bé-ing of óne súbstance
l s F S l d t-s l f S m s
with the Fá-ther: By whóm all thíngs were máde. Who for
L S d d r m f s l d t-s L S
ús mén, and for oúr sal-vá-tion, came dówn from héaven,
s m d r d m r-m s l S l d
*And was in-cár-nate by the Hó-ly Ghóst of the
t s L S d m F S m r-f m-d-r d D
Vír-gin Má-ry: And was máde mán, And was crú-ci-fied

**The following phrase may be sung in harmony, if desired:–*

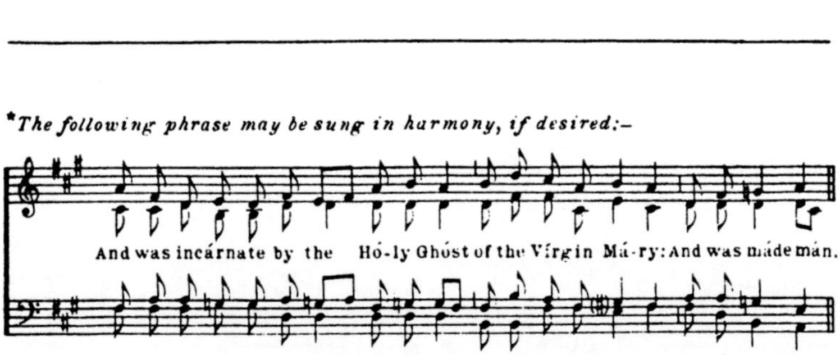
And was incárnate by the Hó-ly Ghóst of the Vírgin Má-ry: And was máde mán.

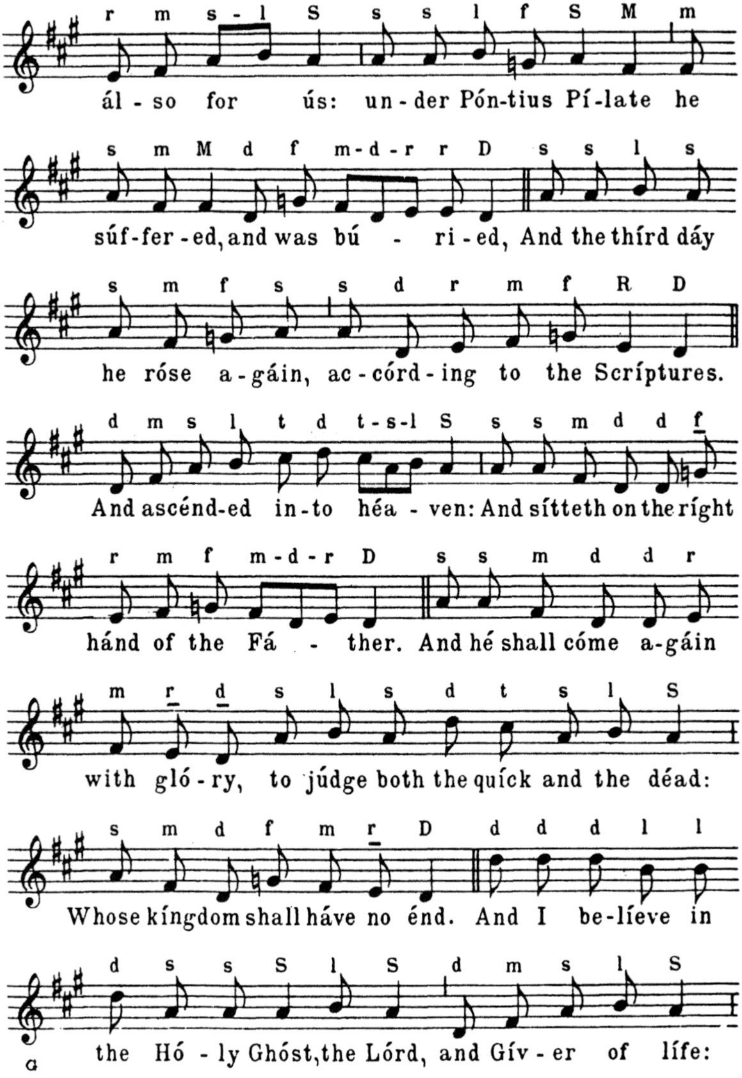
r m s - l S s s l f S M m
ál - so for ús: un - der Pón-tius Pí-late he
s m M d f m-d-r r D s s l s
súf-fer-ed, and was bú - ri-ed, And the thírd dáy
s m f s s d r m f R D
he róse a-gáin, ac-córd-ing to the Scríptures.
d m s l t d t-s-l S s s m d d f
And ascénd-ed in-to héa - ven: And sítteth on the ríght
r m f m-d-r D s s m d d r
hánd of the Fá - ther. And hé shall cóme a-gáin
m r d s l s d t s l S
with gló-ry, to júdge both the quíck and the déad:
s m d f m r D d d d l l
Whose kíngdom shall háve no énd. And I be-líeve in
d s s S l S d m s l S
a the Hó - ly Ghóst, the Lórd, and Gív-er of lífe:

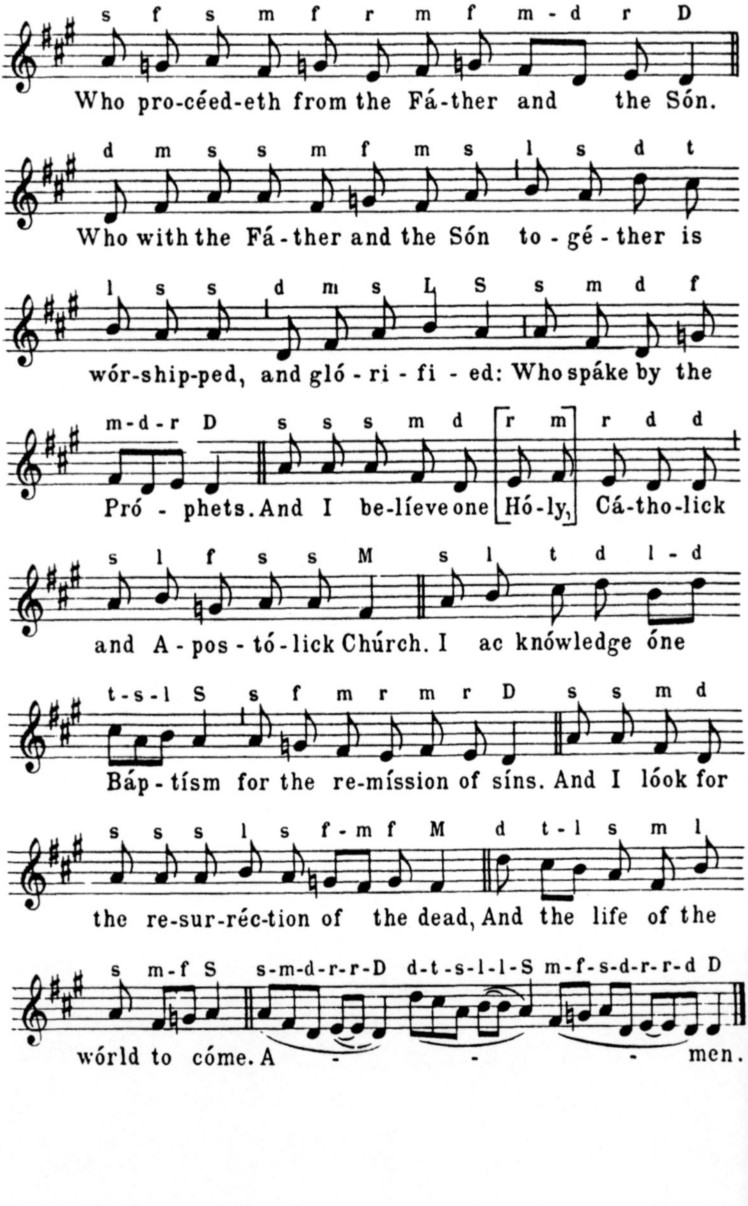
Who pro-céed-eth from the Fá-ther and the Són.
Who with the Fá-ther and the Són to-gé-ther is
wór-ship-ped, and gló-ri-fi-ed: Who spáke by the
Pró-phets. And I be-líeve one Hó-ly, Cá-tho-lick
and A-pos-tó-lick Chúrch. I ac knówledge óne
Báp-tísm for the re-míssion of síns. And I lóok for
the re-sur-réc-tion of the dead, And the life of the
wórld to cóme. A - - - men.

CREDO–IV
(Cardinalis)

Mode I

15th century

♪ = 144
s m f r S L r l s f m-r-d R
I be-líeve in óne Gód, the Fá-ther Al-mígh - ty,
m s l t d t-l-s l t d t d
Má-ker of héa-ven and éarth, and of áll thíngs
t l s t d t l-s L l s f m-r-d
ví-si-ble and in-ví-si - ble. And in óne Lórd
r m-f M m s l t d t t l-s L
Jé-sus Chríst, the ón-ly be-gót-ten Són of Gód.
l t d r d T L r l s-f M r d-m
Be-gót-ten of his Fá-ther be-fóre all wórlds. Gód of
S-L t-d t-l-s L s f m f m r-d R
Gód, Líght of Líght, Vé-ry Gód of vé-ry Gód.
G*

l s l d - t L s l l l s f
Be - gót-ten, not máde, Bé - ing of óne súb-stance
m r d - r - m M m s - l r s f - m R
with the Fá - ther: By whóm all things were máde.
l t d - t L s l r m F S s f
Who for ús mén, and for óur sal-vá-tion,came dówn
m - r - d R R r d r d - t l s d
from héa-ven. * And was in - cár - nate by the
t l - s L l s l s F M s m f - m R
Hó-ly Ghóst of the Vír-gin Má-ry: And was máde mán.

* *The following phrase may be sung in harmony, if desired:—*

And was in-cár-nate by the Hó-ly Ghóst of the Vír-gin Má-ry: And was made mán.

r d r - f - m r f s l d t - l - s L
And was crú - ci - fi - ed ál - so for ús:
r m f s f - m - r · D r f m m f
un - der Pón tius Pí - late he súf-fer - ed and
r m r - d R r d r d t l s L
was bú - ri - ed. And the thírd dáy he rose a - gain,
l s l s f m - r - d R r m f s
ac-córd-ing to the Scríp - tures. And as-cénd-ed
f s - l L l l s l t d t l t
in - to héaven: And sít-teth on the ríght hand of the
s - l L r d t l s l s d - t L
Fá - ther. And hé shall cóme a-gain with gló - ry,
s l s - f - m r m f r M l t d t
to júdge both the quíck and the déad: Whose kíngdom shall
l S L l s l r m f s s l s f - m
havé no énd. And Í be-líeve in the Hó - ly Ghóst, the Lórd,

r m f s M - R r m f m f r m f m
and Gív-er of Lífe: Who pro-céedeth from the Fá-ther and
r - d R l f s l t d t L l s l
the Són. Who with the Fá-ther and the Són to-géth-er
t d t L t l s f - s M m f s m
is wór-ship-ped, and glo-ri - fi - ed Who spáke by the
f - m R r r d t l l l t d r
Pró - phets. And I be-líeve one Hó - ly, Cá-tho-lick
d - t l s f s M r l s l d - t l - s F
and Ap-os-tó-lick Church. I acknówledge óne Báp-tism
r f s f - m f m - r - d R l t d r
for the re - mís - sion of síns. And I lóok for
r m r d t - l d t - l - s L l s f m r
the re-sur-réc-tion of the déad, And the lífe of the
m-r d R f-s-L-R f-s-l-s-F-M s-f-m-r-m-r-d R
wórld to cóme. A - - - - men.

CREDO V
(Monastic)

Mode VIII 13th Century

s l d r d - t L - S l d l s m-f - s S
♪ = 144
I be-líeve in óne Gód, the Fá-ther Al-mígh - ty,
s l d d r d - t L - S s l d d
Má-ker of héa-ven and éarth, and of áll thíngs
r d d l s m f - s S s l d d
ví - si-ble, and in - ví - si - ble. And in óne Lórd
r d - t L - S s l d d l s m f - s S
Jé - sus Chríst, the ón-ly-be-gót-ten Són of Gód.
s l d r d - t l s s m f - s S s l
Be-gót-ten of his Fá-ther be-fóre all wórlds. Gód of
D r d - t L - S d d l s m f - s S
Gód, Líght of Líght, Vé - ry Gód of vé - ry Gód,

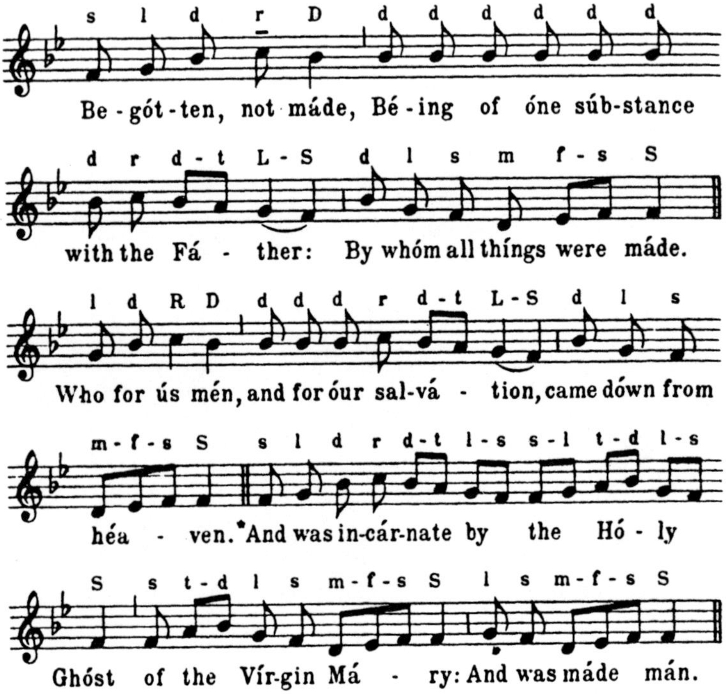
s l d r D d d d d d d
Be - gót - ten, not máde, Bé - ing of óne súb-stance
d r d - t L - S d l s m f - s S
with the Fá - ther: By whóm all thíngs were máde.
l d R D d d d r d - t L - S d l s
Who for ús mén, and for óur sal-vá - tion, came dówn from
m - f - s S s l d r d - t l - s s - l t - d l - s
héa - ven. *And was in-cár-nate by the Hó - ly
S s t - d l s m - f - s S l s m - f - s S
Ghóst of the Vír-gin Má - ry: And was máde mán.

* *The following phrase may be sung in harmony if desired:—*

And was in-cár-nate by the Hó - ly Ghóst of the Vír-gin Má - ry: And was máde mán.

s l d d d d d d d R
And was crú - ci - fi - ed ál - so for ús:
d d d r d - t L - S s l d d l s
un-der Pón-tius Pí - late he súf-fer-ed, and was
m f - s S s l d d d r d - t L - S
bú - ri - ed, And the thírd dáy he róse a - gáin,
s l d l s m - f - s S s l d d
ac-córd-ing to the Scríp - tures. And as-cénd-ed
d r d - t L - S s l d d d d d l s
in - to héa - ven: And sít-teth on the right hánd of the
m - f - s S s l d d d d d R D
Fá - ther. And hé shall cóme a-gáin with gló - ry,
d d d d d r d - t L - S s l d l
to júdge both the quíck and the déad: Whose kíngdom shall
s m - f - s S s l d d d d d d D d R
háve no énd. And I be-líeve in the Hó-ly Ghóst, the Lórd,

d d r d - t L S s l d d d d l s m
and Gív-er of life: Who pro-céed-eth from the Fáther and
f - s S s l d d d d d R d d d
the Són. Who with the Fáther and the Són to-géth-er
d d d d d d r d - t L S l d l s
is wór-shipped and gló-ri-fi - ed: Who spáke by the
m - f - s S s l d d d d d r d d
Pró - phets. And I be-líeve one Hó-ly Cá-tho-lick
d l s m f - s S s l d d r
and A-pos-tó-lick Church. I ac-knów-ledge óne
d - t L - S s l d l s m - f - s S
Báp - tism for the re-mís-sion of síns.
s l d d d d d d d r d - t L - S
And I lóok for the re-sur-réc-tion of the déad,
s l d l s m f - s S f - l - t - l - s F - S
And the lífe of the wórld to cóme. A - - men

CREDO VI
(Merbecke)

Mode I 16th century

l l d r R M m m m f s m
I be-líeve in óne Gód, the Fá-ther Al-mígh-ty,
r d r m m d T l t d r
Má - ker of héa-ven and éarth, and of áll thíngs
r t t d t l l L d d r m
ví - si - ble, and in - ví - si - ble And in óne Lórd
f r M l m m f s m l l S
Jé- sus Chríst,the ón - ly - be - gót - ten Són of Gód,
m m m d r m l t d l L
Be - gót - ten of his Fá-ther be - fóre all wórlds.
m r M m r M d r m s f f M
Gód of Gód, Líght of Líght, Vé - ry Gód of vé - ry Gód,

d r r t D l l t d r l
Be-gót-ten, not máde, Bé-ing of óne súb-stance
r d T L m r d s f M
with the Fá-ther; By whóm all thíngs were máde.
d r M D l d r t d l m m
Who for ús mén, and for óur sal-vá-tion,came dówn
r M l t d r r r r
from héaven,* And was in-cár-nate by the
m f S m m r d F M d r M D
Hó-ly Ghóst of the Vír-gín Má-ry: And was máde mán.

*The following phrase may be sung in harmony, if desired:—

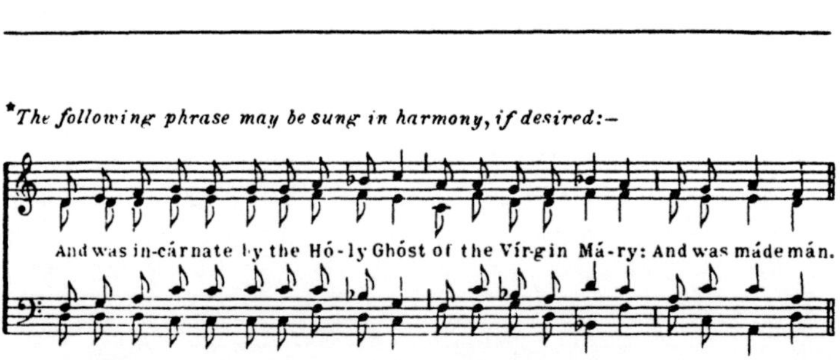
And was in-cárnate by the Hó-ly Ghóst of the Vír-gin Má-ry: And was máde mán.

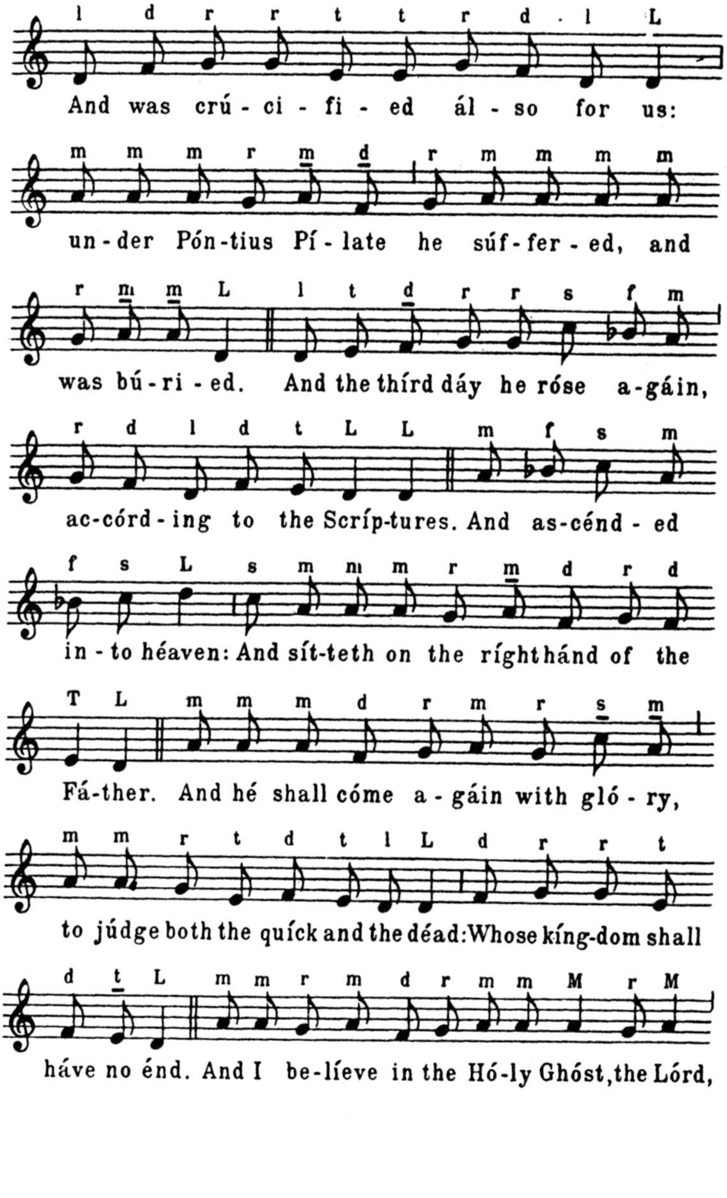
And was crú-ci-fi-ed ál-so for us:
un-der Pón-tius Pí-late he súf-fer-ed, and
was bú-ri-ed. And the thírd dáy he róse a-gáin,
ac-córd-ing to the Scríp-tures. And as-cénd-ed
in-to héaven: And sít-teth on the ríght hánd of the
Fá-ther. And hé shall cóme a-gáin with gló-ry,
to júdge both the quíck and the déad: Whose kíng-dom shall
háve no énd. And I be-líeve in the Hó-ly Ghóst, the Lórd,

f s s m M l t d r m f s m l
and Gí-ver of lífe: Who pro-céed-eth from the Fá-ther and
l S m m m s f m r m f m m
the Són. Who with the Fá - ther and the Són to - gé-ther
d r r t d t l L d r m f
is wór-ship-ped and gló - ri - fied: Who spáke by the
R D m l l s m r m f r r
Próphets. And I be-líeve one Hó-ly, Cá-tho-lick
d r m m m M d d r d
and A - pos - tó - lick Chúrch. I ac - knów - ledge
r m m l d t d l t L
one Báp-tism for the re - mís - sion of síns.
d r m r r m f s f - m r r D
And I loók for the re - sur - réc - tion of the déad,
m m s m r d t L S L
And the life of the wórld to cóme. A - men.

CREDO VII
(Ambrosian)

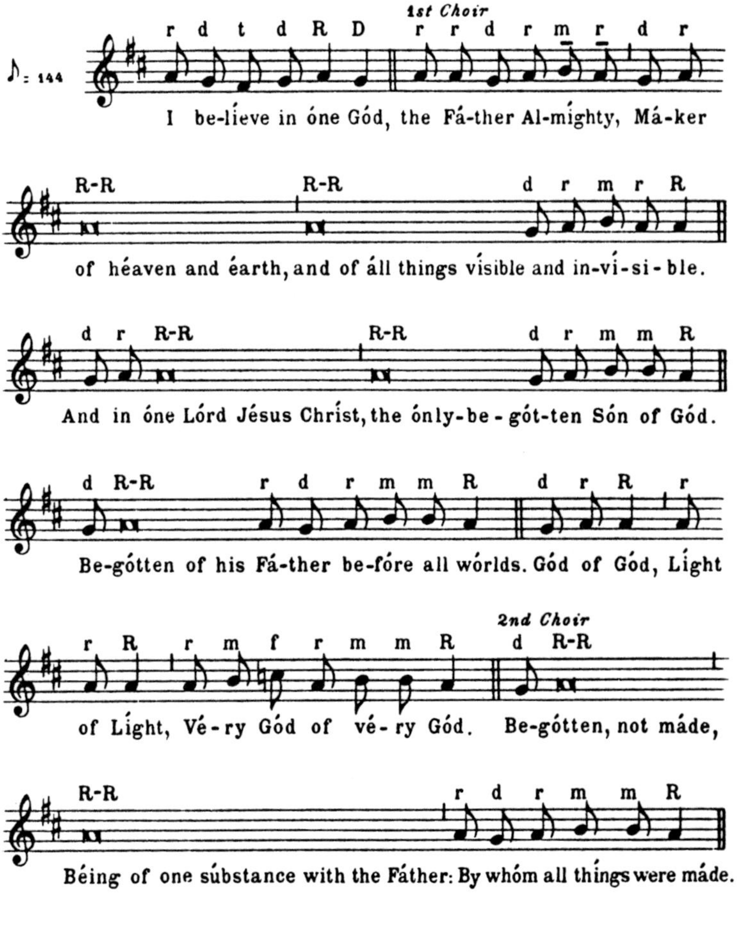
♪ = 144
1st Choir
I be-líeve in óne Gód, the Fá-ther Al-míghty, Má-ker
of héaven and éarth, and of áll things vísible and in-ví-si-ble.
And in óne Lórd Jésus Christ, the ónly-be-gót-ten Són of Gód.
Be-gótten of his Fá-ther be-fóre all wórlds. Gód of Gód, Líght
2nd Choir
of Líght, Vé-ry Gód of vé-ry Gód. Be-gótten, not máde,
Béing of one súbstance with the Fáther: By whóm all thíngs were máde.

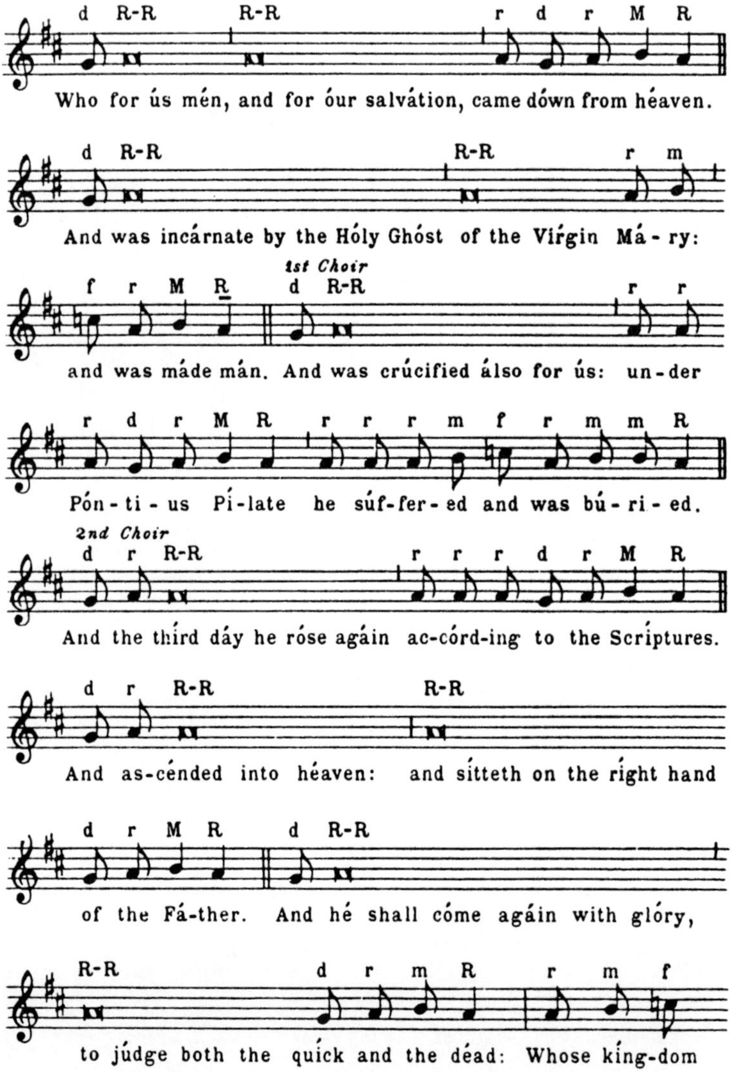
d R-R R-R r d r M R
Who for ús mén, and for óur salvátion, came dówn from héaven.
d R-R R-R r m
And was incárnate by the Hóly Ghóst of the Vírgin Má - ry:
1st Choir
f r M R d R-R r r
and was máde mán. And was crúcified álso for ús: un-der
r d r M R r r r m f r m m R
Pón - ti - us Pí-late he súf-fer-ed and was bú - ri - ed.
2nd Choir
d r R-R r r r d r M R
And the thírd dáy he róse agáin ac-córd-ing to the Scríptures.
d r R-R R-R
And as-cénded into héaven: and sítteth on the ríght hand
d r M R d R-R
of the Fá-ther. And hé shall cóme agáin with glóry,
R-R d r m R r m f
to júdge both the quíck and the déad: Whose kíng-dom

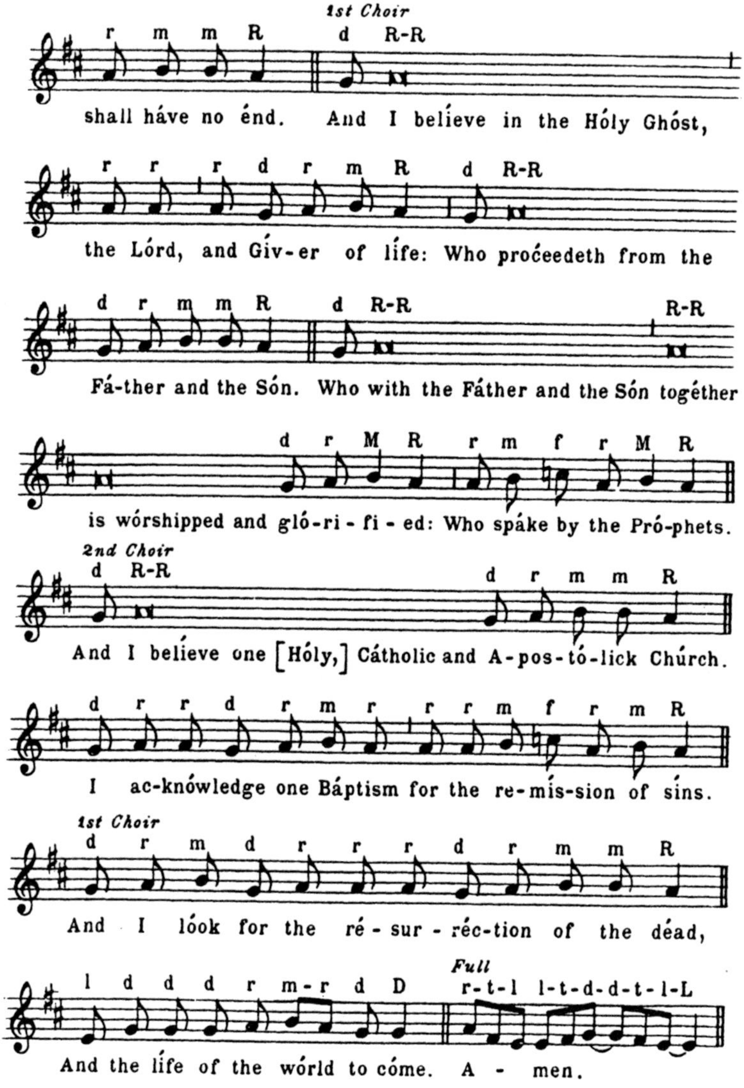
1st Choir
r m m R d R-R
shall háve no énd. And I belíeve in the Hóly Ghóst,
r r r d r m R d R-R
the Lórd, and Gív-er of lífe: Who procéedeth from the
d r m m R d R-R R-R
Fá-ther and the Són. Who with the Fáther and the Són togéther
d r M R r m f r M R
is wórshipped and gló-ri-fi-ed: Who spáke by the Pró-phets.
2nd Choir
d R-R d r m m R
And I belíeve one [Hóly,] Cátholic and A-pos-tó-lick Chúrch.
d r r d r m r r r m f r m R
I ac-knówledge one Báptism for the re-mís-sion of síns.
1st Choir
d r m d r r r d r m m R
And I lóok for the ré-sur-réc-tion of the déad,
Full
l d d d r m-r d D r-t-l l-t-d-d-t-l-L
And the lífe of the wórld to cóme. A - men.

CREDO VIII
(Dumont)

Mode VI 17th century

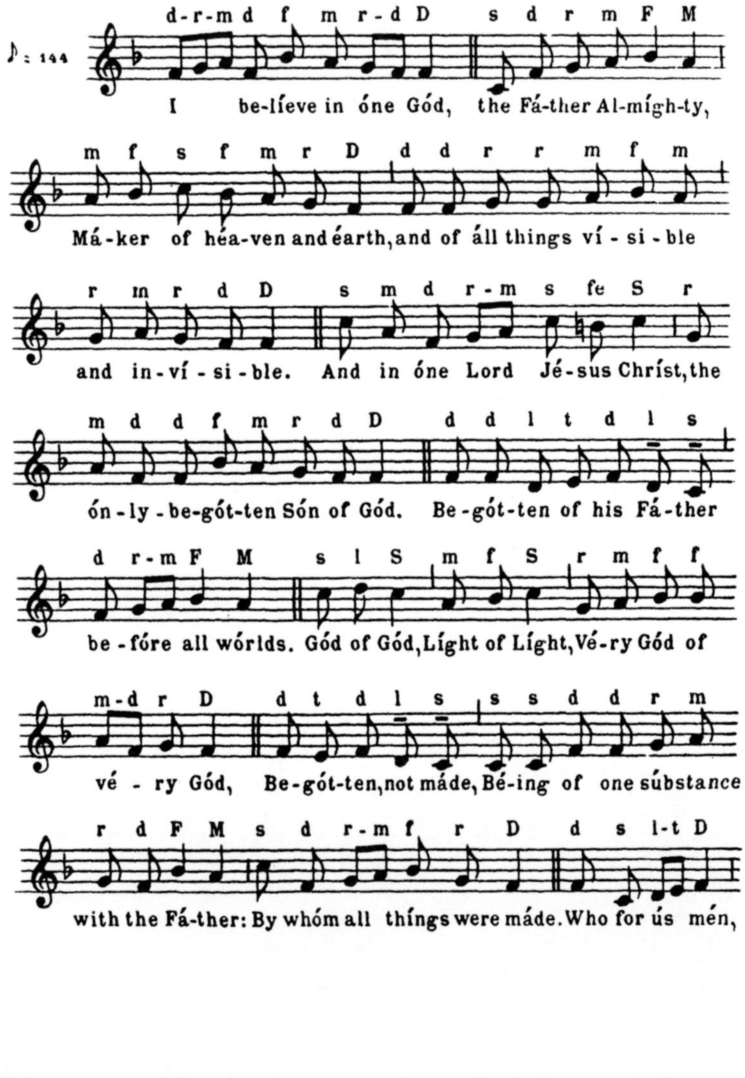
♪ = 144
d-r-m d f m r-d D s d r m F M
I be-líeve in óne Gód, the Fá-ther Al-mígh-ty,
m f s f m r D d d r r m f m
Má-ker of héa-ven and éarth, and of áll things ví - si - ble
r m r d D s m d r-m s fe S r
and in-ví - si - ble. And in óne Lord Jé-sus Chríst, the
m d d f m r d D d d l t d l s
ón - ly - be-gót-ten Són of Gód. Be-gót-ten of his Fá-ther
d r-m F M s l S m f S r m f f
be - fóre all wórlds. Gód of Gód, Líght of Líght, Vé-ry Gód of
m-d r D d t d l s s s d d r m
vé - ry Gód, Be-gót-ten, not máde, Bé-ing of one súbstance
r d F M s d r-m f r D d s l-t D
with the Fá-ther: By whóm all thíngs were máde. Who for ús mén,

d r m r f m s m-r d R D d d d
and for óur sal-vá-tion, came dówn from héaven. And was in -
l s d d m f S s l s m F M
-cár-nate by the Hó - ly Ghóst, of the Vír-gin Má - ry:
r m R D d d s s m r m d f M
and was máde mán. And was crú-ci - fi - ed ál - so for ús:
d d d t d l s d r r r m r
un - der Pón - ti - us Pí - late he súf - fer - ed and was
s fe S s s l s s d r M d f m r
bú - ri - ed. And the thírd dáy he róse a-gáin, ac-córd-ing to
d R D s d r m s f M d d d
the Scríp-tures. And as-cénd-ed in - to héaven: And sít-teth
m f s s s s L S s s f m
on the ríght hand of the Fá - ther. And hé shall cóme
d r m f s d d l r t d l S
a-gáin with gló - ry to júdge both the quíck and the déad:

d r m s f - m R D d d r m d r
Whose kíng-dom shall háve no énd. And Í be-líeve in the
m f S l S s m d r D s s m d r
Hó - ly Ghóst, the Lórd and Gív-er of lífe: Who pro-céedeth from
m f m r d D d l s d d l t d
the Fá-ther and the Són. Who with the Fá-ther and the Són
d d d r m m r m d r - m R D d r
to - gé-ther is wór-ship-ped and gló - ri - fi - ed: Who spáke
m d F M m m s s s s m d r m
by the Pró-phets. And Í be-líeve one Hó - ly, Cá-tho-lick
d m f s l S d d l s d R D d d
and A-pos - tó-lick Church. I ac-knówledge one Báptism for the
r m s fe S s s l s m f s s r
re-mís-sion of síns. And I lóok for the ré - sur - réc - tion
m f M d d f r r m f S d-r f-m r-d-r D
of the déad, And the lífe of the wórld to cóme. A - men.

Missa pro defunctis

INTROIT *Requiem æternam* **MODE VI**

d - d - r - D d - r - m m - r - r - d - r r - d d - r - m m - r
Rést * e - - tér - - nal gránt un
m m - s - m - r - m - f - m - r d - r - m - r - d - r R - D
- to thém, O Lórd :
m - r m m - r - d m r - m r - d d m - r - m - s - m -
and may líght per - pé - tu - al shíne
- r - m - f - m - r d d - r - m - r - d - r R - D
up - ón them.
d - r r - d r - m m m m m R M d r - m m
Ps. Thóu, O Gód, art práis - ed in Sý - on; and ún - to
m m m m m m m m m r f r M
thée shall the vów be per - fórm - ed in Je - rú - sa - lem :
d r - m m m m m m m m d r - m R D
thóu that héar - est the práyer, un - to thée shall all flésh come.

Repeat Introit Rest eternal.

or the following INTROIT (alternative setting).

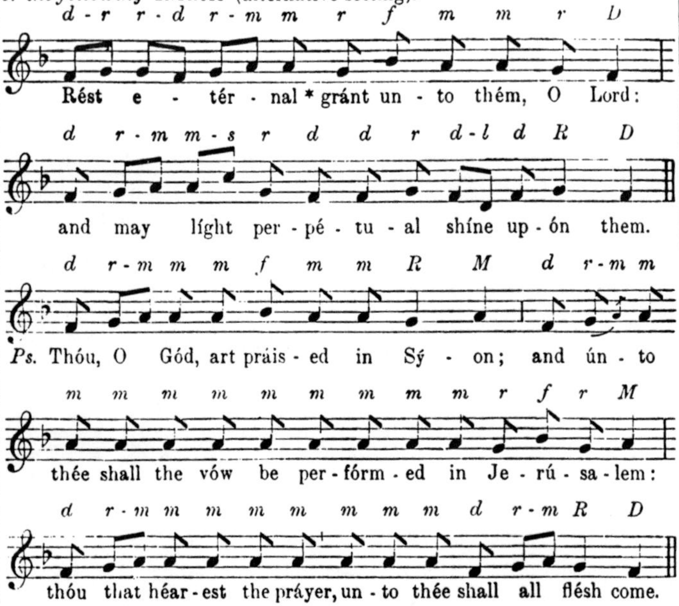
Rést e - tér - nal * gránt un - to thém, O Lord:
and may líght per - pé - tu - al shíne up - ón them.
Ps. Thóu, O Gód, art práis - ed in Sý - on; and ún - to
thée shall the vów be per - fórm - ed in Je - rú - sa - lem:
thóu that héar - est the práyer, un - to thée shall all flésh come.

Repeat Introit Rest eternal.

KYRIE ELEISON — MODE VI

Ký - - ri - e * e - - - - lé - i - son. iij.
Lórd, * have mér - cy. iij.
Chrí - - ste e - - - - lé - i - son. iij
Chríst, have mér - - cy. iij.
Ký - - ri - e e - - - - lé - i - son. ij.
Lórd, have mér - - cy. ij

Ký - ri - e * e - - lé - i - son.
Lórd, * have mér - cy.

GRADUAL *Requiem æternam* **MODE II**

Rést * e - tér - - - - - nal gránt
un - to thém, O Lórd:
and may líght per - pé - - -
- - - - - - - tu - al
shíne up - ón them.
℣. The ríghteous shall be hád in ev - - - - - - -

- d - d - r - m - r - M d - m - f - r - t - d - l - s - l - t - l - s - L r - m - f - m
- f - m - r - m m - r r - m - f - m - r - m - f - m - r r - m m m - d - m - r - d -
er - lást ing re - mém
- d - l d - d - l - D - d - d - d - l d - r - m - r - d - m - r - d - r - l L
brance :
d - d d d d d d d - r r - d - t - s - l - d - t - s - l - d - t - r - m - d - l
he will nót be a-fráid of á
l - d - l - s - l - d - d - l - d - d - t - l - d - s - S - F f - s - l - d - t - l - t
ny * é
s - l d - l - d - r r - m - d - t - d - r s - l - d - d - m - r - d - t - l - t - d - L
vil ti dings.

or the following GRADUAL (alternative setting).

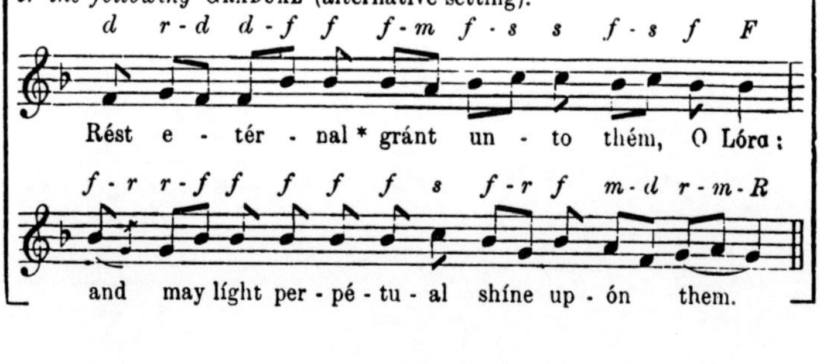
d r - d d - f f f - m f - s s f - s f F
Rést e - tér - nal * gránt un - to thém, O Lórd :
f - r r - f f f f f s f - r f m - d r - m - R
and may líght per - pé - tu - al shíne up - ón them.

d r-d d-f f f f f f f f-m f-s s f-s F
℣. The rígh-teous shall be hád in ev-er-lást-ing re-mém-brance:
f-r r-f f f f f f f s f-r f m-d r-m-R
he will nót be a-fráid of á-ny é-vil tí-dings.

TRACT *Absolve Domine* MODE VIII

s-l-t-l s-l-l-s s-d-d-r-l s-f-s-l-l-s s s-d
Ab - sólve, * O Lórd, the sóuls
d d d l-d d d t-r-m-d-d-l d-l-l-s-l-s-l-s-
of áll the fáith-ful de-párt - - ed
-d-d-l-d-s-S-F f l-d t-s-l s-l-d-t-d D-l-t-d
from év-ery bónd of
d-d-d-t-l-t-l-s-L-S s s-d d d d t-r-m-d-d-l
sín. ℣. And by the hélp of thy
d-l-l-s-l-s-d-d-l-d-s-S-F f f l-d t-s-t s-f s-s
gráce may they be á - ble to
s S s s s-l-d-t-d d D-l-t-d d-d-d-t-l-t-l-s-L-S
escápe the a-véng - ing júdge - ment.

s s-d t-r-m-d-d-l-d-l-l-s-l-s-d-d-l-d-s-S-F
℣. And en - jóy
s s s l-s-l-t-d s-l-s-f F-l-t-d-r d
the blíss of ev - - - - er - - lást - - ing
d-t-d-l-s-s-s-l-s-s-f-S d-d-d-r-d-t-l-
líght.
-l-s-l-d-t-l-s-s-l-F l-t-d-t-l-t-l-L-S

or the following Tract (alternative setting).

s l-s s-d d d d d d d d-t d-r r d-r D
Ab - sólve, O Lórd,* the sóuls of áll the fáith - ful de - párt - ed :
d-d-t s-l d-l l s S s l-s s-d d d d d
from év - ery bónd of sín. ℣. And by the hélp of thy gráce
d d d d d d d d d d-t d-r r d-r D
may they be á - ble to es-cápe the a - véng - ing júdge-ment :
d-l l-d d d d d-d-t s-l d-t l s S
and en - jóy the blíss of ev - er - lást-ing líght.

SEQUENCE *Dies iræ dies illa* MODE 1

f m f r m d R R f f-s f-m r-d
1. Dáy of wráth and dóom im-pénd-ing, Dá - vid's wórd with
2. Ó, what féar man's bó- som rén- deth, Whén from héav'n the
m f M R l d-r r r-d m f M R
Sí- byl's blénd - ing! Héav'n and éarth in ásh - es énd - ing!
Júdge de - scén - deth, On whose sén - tence áll de- pén - deth!
l d d t-s-l l-s-f s l L-R f m f r
3. Wóndrous sóund the trúm - pet flíng - eth, Thró' earth's sé-pul -
4. Déath is strúck, and ná - ture quá - king, Áll cre - á - tion
m d R R f s-l l-s-f m-r-d m f M R
- chres it ríng - eth, Áll be - fóre the thróne it bríng-eth.
is a - wá - king, To its Júdge an án - swer má - king.
l s-f s l-r r-d l d-r R f-m r d l d r
5. Ló! the bóok ex - áct - ly wórd-ed, Whére-in áll hath béen re -
6. Whén the Júdge his séat at - táin-eth, And each híd-den déed ar-
f m-d-R l f s r d r f m-d-R
- córd - ed; Thénce shall júdgement be a - wárd - ed.
ráign - eth, Nó - thing un - a- véng'd re - máin-eth.
f m f r m d R R f f-s f-m r-d
7. Whát shall I, frail mán, be pléad - ing? Whó for mé be
8. Kíng of má - jes - ty tre-mén - dous, Whó dost frée sal -
m f M R l d-r r r-d m f M R
in - ter-céd - ing, Whén the júst are mér-cy néed - ing?
- vá - tion sénd us, Fóunt of pí - ty thén be-fríend us!

l d d t-s-l l-s-f s l L-R f m f r
9. Thínk, kind Jé-su!— mý sal-vá-tion Cáus'd thy wóndrous
10. Fáint and wéa-ry thóu hast sóught me, On the Cróss of
m d R R f s-l l-s-f m-r-d m f M R
Ín-car-ná-tion; Léave me nót to ré-pro-bá-tion.
súf-f'ring bóught me; Shāll such gráce be váin-ly bróught me?
l s-f s l-r r-d l .d-r R f-m r d l
11. Rìght-eous Júdge! for sín's pol-lú-tion Gránt thy gíft of
12. Gúilt-y, nów I póur my móan-ing, Áll my sháme with
d r f m-d-R l f s r d r f m-d-R
áb-so-lú-tion, Ére that dáy of ré-tri-bú-tion.
án-guish ówn-ing; Spáre, O Gód, thy súppliant gróaning!
f m f r m d R R f f-s f-m r-d
13. Thróugh the sín-ful wó-man shrí-ven, Thróugh the dý-ing
14. Wórth-less áre my práyers and sigh-ing, Yét, good Lórd, in
m f M R l d r r r-d m f M R
thíef for-gív-en, Thóu to mé a hópe hast gív-en.
gráce com-plý-ing, Rés-cue mé from fíres un-dý-ing.
l d d t-s-l l-s-f s l L-R f m f r
15. Wíth thy shéep a pláce pro-víde me, Fróm the góats a
16. Whén the wíck-ed áre con-fóund-ed, Dóom'd to flámes of
m d R R r s-l l-s-f m-r-d m f M R
fár di-vide me, To thy right hand dó thou guíde me.
woe un-bóund-ed, Cáll me, with thy Sáints surróund-ed.

17. Lów I knéel, with héart sub - mís - sion; Sée, like ásh - es,
my con - trí - tion! Hélp me in my lást con - dí - tion!
18. Áh! that dáy of téars and móurning! From the dúst of éarth
re - túrn - ing, 19. Mán for júdgement must pre - páre him; Spáre, O
Gód, in mér - cy spáre him. 20. Lórd, all pí - tying, Jé - su blést,
gránt them thíne e - tér - nal rést. A - - - men.

OFFERTORY *Domine Jesu Christe* MODE II

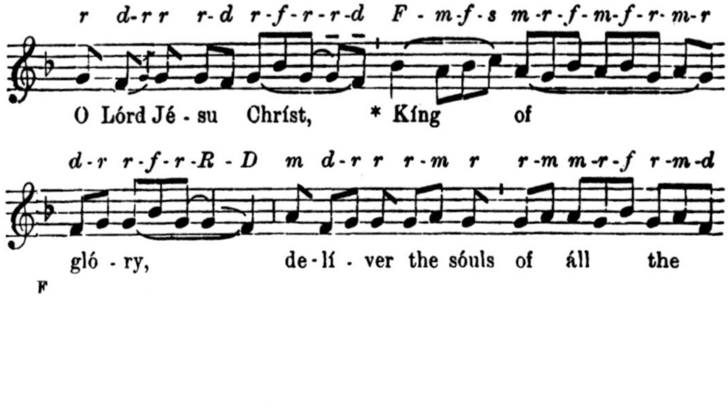
O Lórd Jé - su Chríst, * Kíng of
gló - ry, de - lí - ver the sóuls of áll the

d d-r-f m-f r-m-r R r d-r r r-m-f-r R m d
fáith-ful de - párt - ed from the hánd of héll, and from
r f m r r-m-r R m d r f-m r m-r s s-s-f-r-d
the pít of de - strúc- tion : de - lí -ver them from the lí - on's
r-m-f-M d r f m-r m-f-r d-r R r r r d-l d
móuth, that the gráve de - vóur them nót ; that they gó not dówn
d r f r-m M-r-m f-r R r R-m-f-s f-m r-m m
to the réalms of dárk - - ness : but let Mí - cha - el,
m m-r r-m-f-m r r-m-r d-r R r f-m f f-s
the hó - ly stán - dard béar - er, make spéed to re -
s-s-f-r-d R-M d d-m M-r-m-f m-r d d-m-f-r R
- stóre them to the bríght - ness of gló - ry :
r d-l-d r-m m-r f f-m r-m r R-D f-s m-r f-s-f-r-
which thou pró - mis-edst in á - ges pást to A - - -
- r-D-r-f-m-f-s-m r-f-m r-m-d d-l d d-r-m-f-r R
- - - - - - - - - bra - ham and his séed.

d r-f f-f-m r-d r-f-f-f-m d r-f f r-m-r-d
℣. Sác-ri - fice and prayer do we óf-fer
m-r m-f m-r d-r R r R-m-f-s f-m r-m M
un - to thée, O Lórd: do thóu ac - cépt them
r d r-f m-f-m R R s-f s-l-s f m-f R
for the sóuls de - párt-ed, in whose mé-mo-ry
r r-d-r f-m r-m r-d D r-m d-l d-r R
we máke this o - blá-tion: and gránt them, Lórd,
f m-r-r-d m-f-s s-s-f m-r m-f-m R r d-l-d
to páss from déath un - to lífe. Which thou
r-m m-r f f-m r-m r R-D f-s m-r-f-s-f-r-
pró - mis-edst in á - ges pást to A - - -
-r-D-r-f-m f-s-m r-f-m r-m-d d-l d d-r-m-f-r R
. . . . bra - ham and his séed.
or the following OFFERTORY (alternative setting).
s-d-t d-r r r r r r r r r r r r r r
O Lórd Jé-su Christ, * King of gló-ry, de - lí-ver the sóuls

of áll the faíth-ful de-párt-ed from the hánd of héll:
and from the pít of de-strúc - tion; De - lí -
- ver them from the lí-on's móuth, that the gráve de-vóur them nót:
that they gó not dówn in-to the réalms of dárk - ness;
But let Mí-cha-el, the hó - ly stándard béarer, make spéed
to restóre them to the bríghtness of gló - ry: which thou
prómisedst in á-ges pást to Á - bra - ham and his séed.
℣. Sác - ri - fice and práyer do we óf-fer un - to thée, O Lórd:

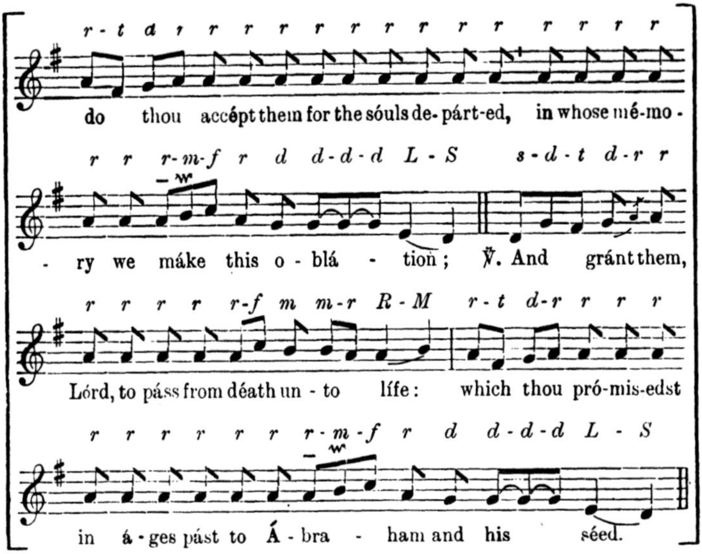
do thou accépt them for the sóuls de- párt-ed, in whose mé-mo -
- ry we máke this o - blá - tion ; ℣. And gránt them,
Lórd, to páss from déath un - to lífe : which thou pró-mis-edst
in á - ges pást to Á - bra - ham and his séed.

SANCTUS

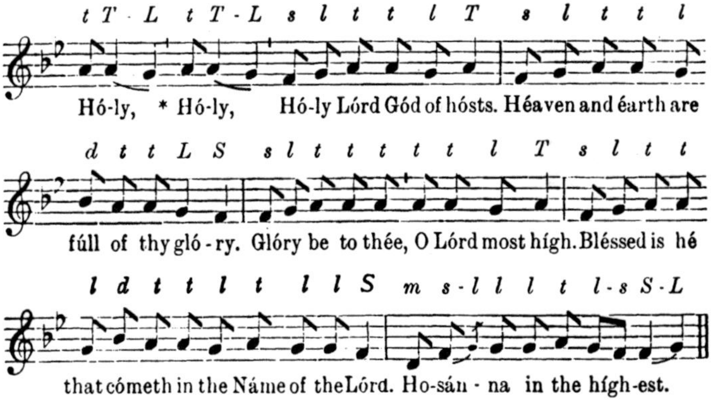
Hó-ly, * Hó-ly, Hó-ly Lórd Gód of hósts. Héaven and éarth are
fúll of thy gló - ry. Glóry be to thée, O Lórd most hígh. Bléssed is hé
that cómeth in the Náme of the Lórd. Ho-sán - na in the hígh-est.

AGNUS DEI

O Lámb of Gód, * that tá - kest a - wáy the síns of the wórld :

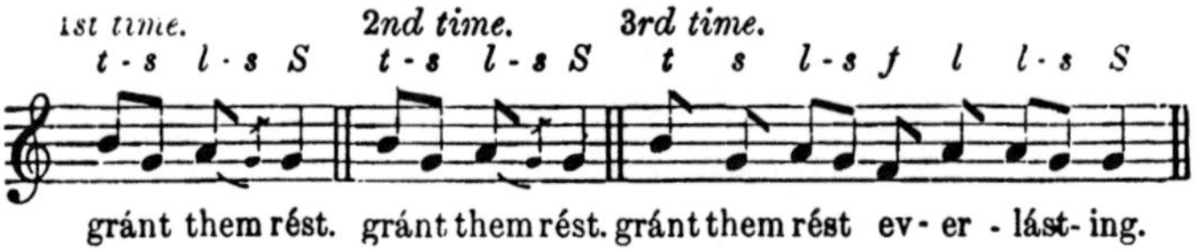
1st time. 2nd time. 3rd time.
t - s l · s S t - s l - s S t s l - s f l l · s S
gránt them rést. gránt them rést. gránt them rést ev - er - lást- ing.

COMMUNION *Lux æterna* **MODE VIII**

s l s - f s - l s l · d t d l - s f · s S
Let líght e - tér - nal * shíne, O Lórd, up - ón them:
l d t d l t d· l s - l - s m f s -l L S
. For éndless á - ges with thy Sáints, for thóu art grá - cious.
s l d d d d r r d D l d
℣. Rést e - tér - nal gránt un - to thém, O Lórd: and may
d d d d d t d L S
líght per - pé - tu - al shíne up - ón them.
l d t d l t d - l s - l - S m f s - l L S
For éndless á - ges with thy Sáints, for thóu art grá- cious.

AT THE END

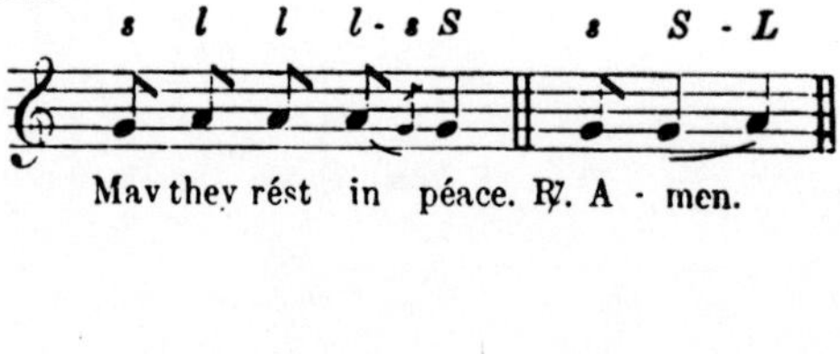
s l l l - s S s S - L
May they rést in péace. ℟. A - men.

THE ABSOLUTIONS

RESPONSARY *Libera me Domine* MODE I

De - lí - ver me, O Lórd, * from déath
e - tér - - nal, in that dáy
tre - mén - - dous: When the héa - vens
and the éarth must páss a - wáy:
When thóu shalt cóme to júdge
the wórld by fíre. ℣. Trémbling
hath laid hóld on me, and féar - ful - ness, while I a-wáit
the síft - ing, and the cóm - ing án - ger.

d - r r m - f - s s - f - m m - s - l - ta - s f m - f r r - m - r d
When the héa - vens and the éarth must páss
r - m - f M - R f m f r m r - d r - m r m f s
a - wáy. ℣. Dáy of móurning, dáy of án - ger, of ca - lá -
s - l s - f r f s - f F m - f s f f - m r - d r f
- mi - ty and mí - se - ry, that gréat dáy and ex - céed-ing
m - r - d R l l - s - l - f - s - l - ta - s - f - m - r m - r r
bít - ter. When thóu shalt cóme
l - s l - d - t - s - s - l - s - f - m - r m - f - s - m - f - m d - f - m - f - s - s - d
to júdge the wórld
r - m - f M - R f r m r m f s - f r - d D f l l - s
by fíre. ℣. Rést e - tér - nal gránt to them, O Lórd : and may líght
f s f - m r r - d m f - m R r r - d r F m - r - m - f - r
per - pé - tu - al shíne up - ón them. De - lí - ver me, O
d - r m - f - s s - f - r f m - r - f - f - r R r - m - d
Lórd, from déath e - tér - - nal in

that day tre - mén - dous: When the héa -
- vens and the éarth must páss a - wáy:
When thóu shalt cóme to júdge
the wórld by fíre.

or the following RESPONSARY (alternative setting).

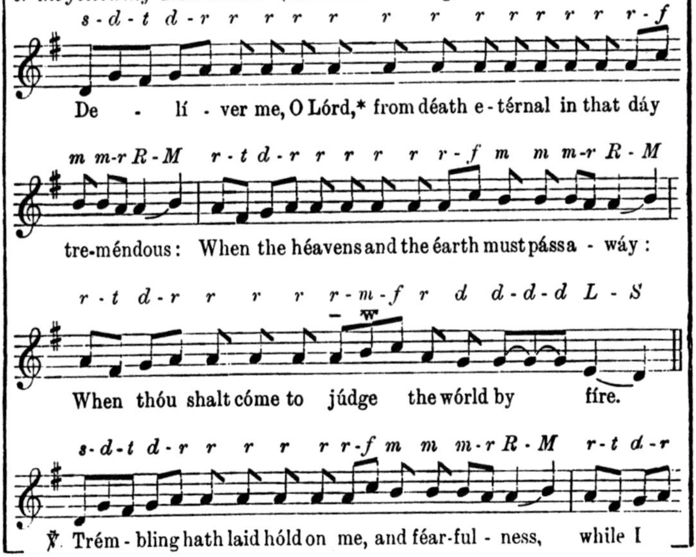
De - lí - ver me, O Lórd,* from déath e - térnal in that dáy
tre-méndous: When the héavens and the éarth must páss a - wáy:
When thóu shalt cóme to júdge the wórld by fíre.
℣. Trém - bling hath laid hóld on me, and féar-ful - ness, while I

r r r r r r r r-f m m-r R-M r-t d-r
a-wáit the síft-ing and the cóm-ing án-ger. When the
r r r r r-m-f r d d-d-d L-S s-d-t d-r
héavens and the éarth must páss a-wáy. ℣. Dáy of
r r r r r r r r r r r-f m m m-r R-M
móurning, dáy of án-ger, of ca-lá-mi-ty and mí-se-ry,
r-t d-r r r r r-f m m-r R-M r-t d-r r r
that gréat dáy and ex-céed-ing bít-ter. When thóu shalt cóme
r r-m-f r d d-d-d L-S s-d-t d-r r r r-f m
to júdge the wórld by fíre. ℣ Rést e-tér-nal gránt to
m m-r R-M r-t d-r r r r r r-m-f r d-d-d L-S
them, O Lórd: and may líght per-pé-tu-al shíne up-ón them.
s-d-t d-r r r r r r r r r r r r r-f m
De-lív-er me, O Lórd, from déath e-tér-nal in that dáy tre-
m-r R-M r-t d-r r r r r r-f m m m-r R M
-men-dous: when the héavens and the éarth must páss a-wáy:

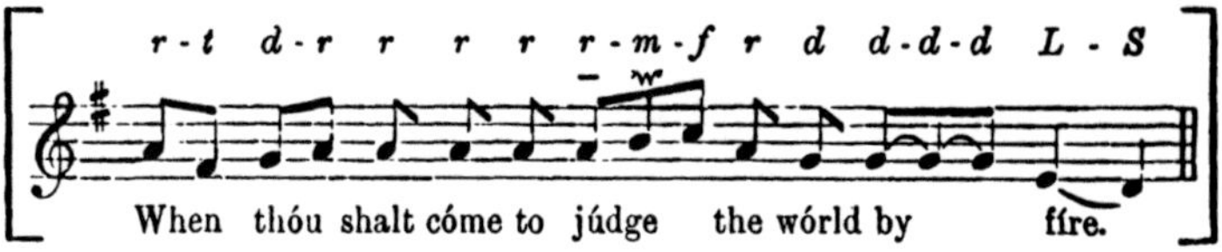
r - t d - r r r r r - m - f r d d - d - d L - S
When thóu shalt cóme to júdge the wórld by fíre.

CANTOR WITH 1ST CHOIR. SECOND CHOIR.

d d d (d) d r-m r R - D d d (d) (d) d r-m r R - D
Ký - ri - e e - lé - i - son. Chrí-ste e - lé - i - son.
Lórd, have mércy up - ón us. Chríst, have mércy up-ón us.

ALL. PRIEST.

m r d (d) m - s - r m r D - T d D L
Ký - ri - e e - lé - i - son. Our Fá - ther.
Lórd, have mér-cy up - ón us.

(*Continued silently.*)

℣. And léad us nót into temptá -	tion.	
℟. But delíver us from é - -	vil.	
℣. From the gátes	of	héll.
℟. Delíver *their* sóul (s),	O	Lórd.
℣. May *they* rést	in	péace.
℟. Amen.		
℣. Lórd, héar	my	práyer.
℟. And let my crý come ún - -	to	thée.
℣. The Lórd be wíth you.		
℟. And wíth thy spírit.		
PRIEST. Let us pray.		
℟. Amen.		
℣. Rést etérnal gránt unto *thém*,	O	Lórd.
℟. And may líght perpétual shíne up-	on	*them*.

s l l l - s S s S - L
May *they* rést in péace. ℟. A - men.

Mass Responses

1.—AT THE COLLECT FOR THE DAY

1.—Festal and Ferial Tones

d d d d D d d d D D
℣. The Lórd be wíth you. ℟. And wíth thy spí - rit.
d d D d d D D D D
Priest. Lét us práy. . . . . wórld with-óut énd. ℟. A - men.

2.—Ancient Tone *ad libitum*

s l s - l l - s S s l s L L
℣. The Lórd be wíth you. ℟. And wíth thy spí - rit.
l s - l L s l l - s S S L
Priest. Lét us práy. . . . wórld with - óut énd. ℟. A - men.

3.—Sarum Tone

l d t - d d - t T l d t - d d - t T
℣. The Lórd be wíth you. ℟. And wíth thy spí - rit.
d t - d D d d d - t T t - d D
Priest. Lét us práy. . . . wórld with - óut énd. ℟. A - men.

II.—AT THE GOSPEL FOR THE DAY

1.

d d d d D d d d D D
℣. The Lórd be wíth you . And wíth thy spí - rit.
D d l d d D d d d d d l D
. . . . ac-córd-ing to Márk. ℟. Gló-ry be to thée, O Lórd.
[at the first vérse.]

2.—Another Tone *ad libitum*

d d l d D d d l D D
℣. The Lórd be wíth you. ℟. And wíth thy spí - rit.
D d d d d d-l L d d d d d l D
. . . . . ac-córd-ing to Mátthew. ℟. Gló-ry be to thée, O Lórd.
[at the first vérse.]

3.—Another Tone *ad libitum*

s l s-l l-s S s l s L L
℣. The Lórd be wíth you. ℟. And wíth thy spí - rit.
L l l l l S l l l l l l S
. . . . . ac-córd-ing to Lúke. ℟. Gló-ry be to thée, O Lórd.
[at the first vérse.]

4.—Sarum Tone

l d t-d d-t T l d t-d d-t T
℣. The Lórd be wíth you. ℟. And wíth thy spí - rit.
D d d d d T* d d d d d d T*
. . . . . ac-córd-ing to Jóhn. ℟. Gló-ry be to thée, O Lórd.
[at the first vérse.]

* *but on Double Feasts these final notes drop a minor third to LA*

III.—BEFORE THE OFFERTORY.

1.—FESTAL AND FERIAL TONES

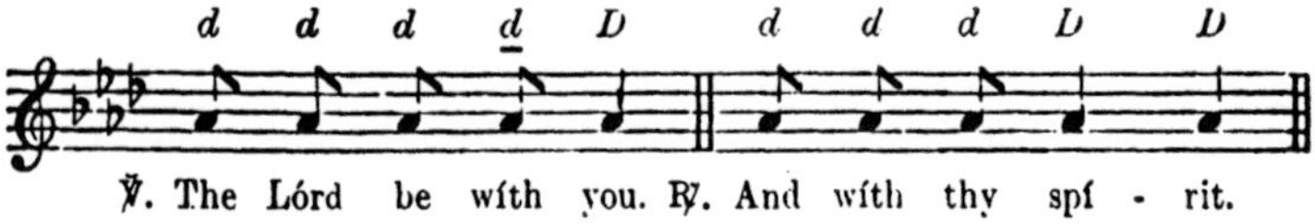
d d d d D d d d D D
℣. The Lórd be wíth you. ℟. And wíth thy spí - rit.

2.—SARUM TONE

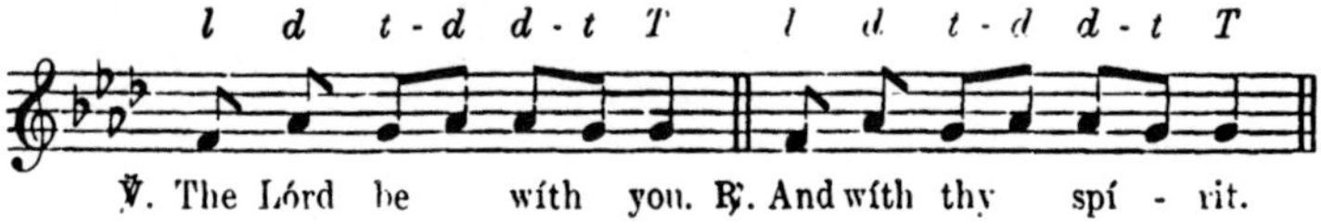
l d t - d d - t T l d t - d d - t T
℣. The Lórd be wíth you. ℟. And wíth thy spí - rit.

IV.—AFTER THE OFFERTORY

or (Sarum Tone)

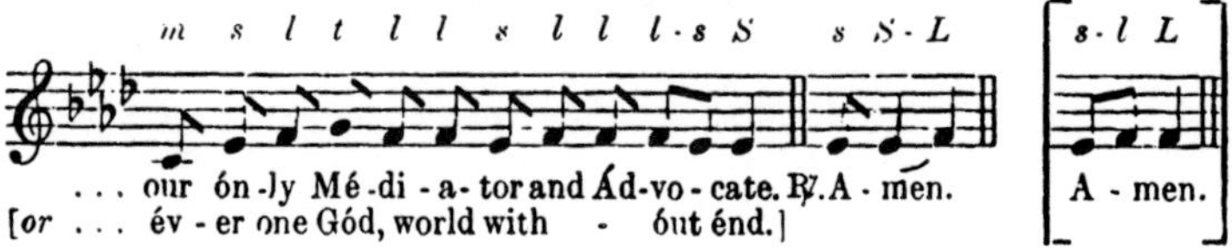
m s l t l l s l l l - s S s S - L
. . . our ón - ly Mé - di - a - tor and Ád - vo - cate. ℟. A - men.
[or . . . év - er one Gód, world with - óut énd.]
s - l L
A - men.

V.—AT THE *SURSUM CORDA*

1.—SOLEMN TONE

d - r m d - r m - r R d - r m d - r m - r R r - m - f m
℣. The Lórd be wíth you. ℟. And wíth thy spi - rit. ℣. Líft up
r - m R - D m r - m - f m m m r - m
your héarts. ℟. We líft them úp un - to
r R - D m - r d m - r - m f - m r - d d - r m
the Lórd. ℣. Lét us give thánks un - to our
r - m R r m f m m r - m r R - D
Lórd Gód. ℟. It is méet and ríght só to dó.

2.—Ferial Tone

d-r m d-r M R d-r m d-r M R f m r-m R-D
℣. The Lórd be wíth you. ℟. And wíth thy spí-rit. ℣. Lift up your héarts.
m f m m r m r R-D f m r m
℟. We lift them úp un-to the Lórd. ℣. Lét us give thánks
m d r M R r m f m r m r R-D
un-to our Lórd Gód. ℟. It is méet and ríght só to dó.

3.—Very Solemn Tone

d-r m-r d-r m-r R d-r m-r d-r m-r R
℣. The Lórd be wíth you. ℟. And wíth thy spí-rit.
D-r-m-f m-r r-m R-D d D-r-m-f m m m-r
℣. Lift up your héarts. ℟. We lift them úp un-
r-m-f r R-D f-m r-d r f-m r-d d-r f
-to the Lórd. ℣. Lét us give thánks un-to our
m-r-m R r m f m m-r r-m-f r R-D
Lórd Gód. ℟. It is méet and ríght só to dó.

1.—Sarum Tone

d-r m d-r m-r R d-r m d-r m-r R r-m-f m
℣. The Lórd be wíth you. ℟. And wíth thy spí - rit. ℣. Líft up
r-m R-D r f m m m r-m r R-D m m m f
your héarts. ℟. We líft them úp un - to the Lórd. ℣. Lét us give thánks
r-d d-r f r-m R r m f m m r-m r R-D
un - to our Lórd Gód. ℟. It is méet and ríght só to dó.

VI.—BEFORE THE *PATER NOSTER*

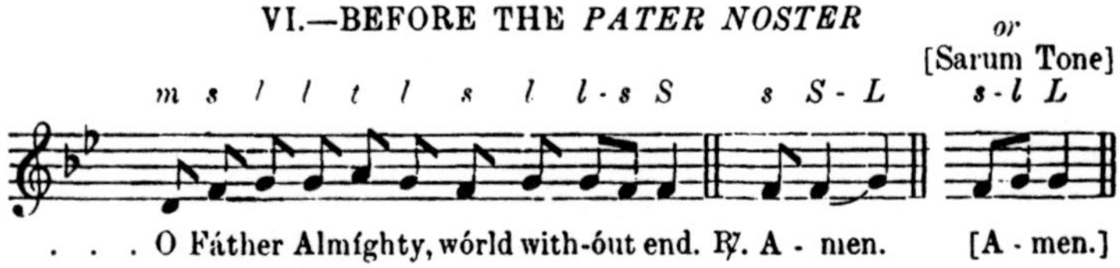
or
[Sarum Tone]
m s l l t l s l l-s S s S-L s-l L
. . . O Fáther Almíghty, wórld with-óut end. ℟. A - men. [A - men.]

(When the *Pater noster* is to be sung to the Ferial Tone the foregoing passage should be one note lower.)

VII.—THE *PATER NOSTER*

1.—Festal Tone.

d-r M M r f m R D m r-d d-r m r-m R
Our Fá - ther, which árt in héa - ven: Hál - low - ed be thý Náme:
m r m R-D m m r m r r-d m r-d d-r
Thy Kíngdom cóme: Thý will be dóne, in éarth as it ís
m r-m R d r m f m r m R-D r m f
in héa - ven. Gíve us this dáy our dái - ly bréad: and for- gíve

us our trés-pass-es, as wé for-gíve them that trés-pass a-gáinst us.
And léad us not ín - to temp - tá - tion. ℟. But de - lív - er us
from é - vil. [For thíne is the Kíng - dom, the pów - er and the
gló - ry, for év - er and év - er. A - men.]

2.—**Ferial Tone**

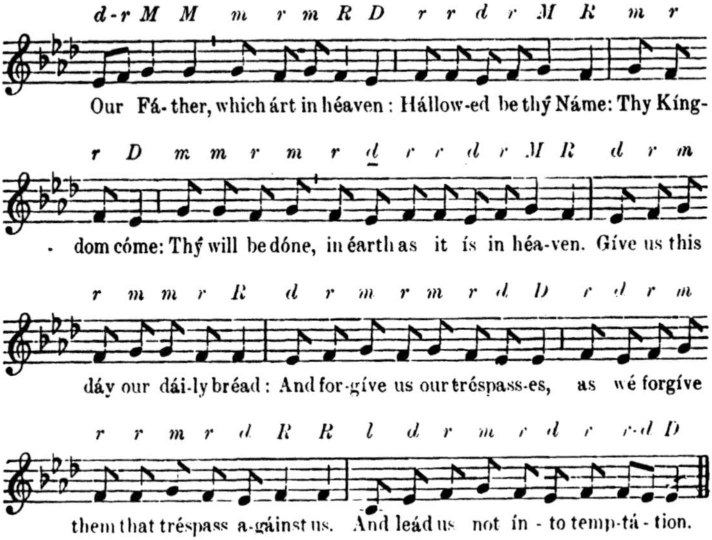
Our Fá- ther, which árt in héaven : Hállow-ed be thý Náme: Thy Kíng-
- dom cóme: Thý will be dóne, in éarth as it ís in héa-ven. Gíve us this
dáy our dái-ly bréad : And for-gíve us our tréspass-es, as wé forgíve
them that tréspass a-gáinst us. And léad us not ín - to temp-tá - tion.

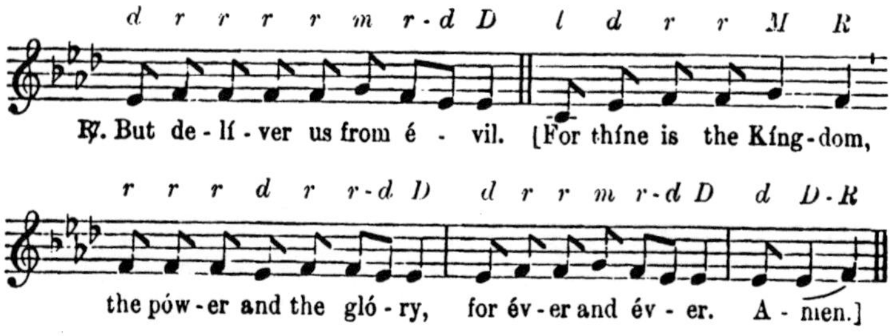
℟. But de - lí - ver us from é - vil. [For thíne is the Kíng - dom,
the pów - er and the gló - ry, for év - er and év - er. A - men.]

3.—Sarum Tone

Our Fá - ther, which árt in heá - ven: Hál - low - ed be thý Náme:
Thy Kíngdom cóme: Thý will be dóne, in éarth as it ís in
heá - ven. Gíve us this dáy our dái - ly breád: And for - gíve us our trés-
- pass - es, as wé for - gíve them that tréspass agáinst us. And léad us not
ín - to temp - tá - tion. ℟. But de - lí - ver us from é - vil. [For thíne is the
Kingdom, the pówer and the gló - ry, for év - er and év - er. A - men.]

VIII.—BEFORE *AGNUS DEI*

l d r m r d r r-d D d D-R
. . . throughóut all á - ges, wórld with - óut énd. ℟. A - men.

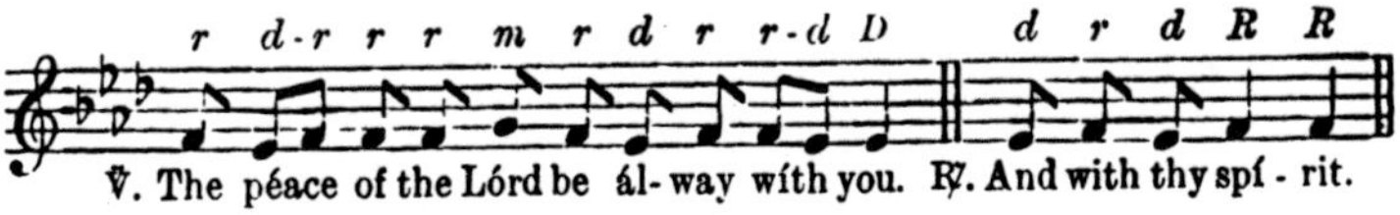
r d-r r r m r d r r-d D d r d R R
℣. The péace of the Lórd be ál- way wíth you. ℟. And with thy spí - rit.

IX.—AT THE END

1 (*a*).—From Holy Saturday to the Saturday before Low Sunday inclusive

s s s l s f s-l L l s-d-t-l-s f-s-l L-S
℟. Thánks be to Gód, al - le - lú - ya, al - le - - lú - ya.

1 (*b*).—From Low Sunday to Ember Saturday in Whitsun-week inclusive

s-t-d-r-d-r-m-r-r-t-r-d-t-l-s l-t-l l S
℟. Thánks be to Gód.
[A - men.]

2.—On Solemn Feasts

s-l-t-T-l-d-t-t-s-l-l-s-f-m-R r-l-l-s-l-d-t l-s-f s-l-s s M
℟. Thánks be to Gód.
[A - men.]

3.—On Solemn Feasts

d-t-s-l-S-m-f-s-s-r-m-r-D d-t-s-l-S-
℟. Thánks
[A -

-m-f-s-s-r-m-r-D d-r-m-f-m r-d D
be to Gód.
men.]

4.—On Double Feasts

l - l - s - L - d - t - l - s - L   l - s - f - r - M   m - s - l - r - m - s - f - m f r R

℟. Thánks be to God.
[A - men.]

5.—On Double Feasts

s - l - t - d - t - l - S - l - t - m - f - m - r - D   s - l - t - d - t - l - S -

℟. Thánks
[A -

- l - l - s - f - m - f s S

be to Gód.
men.]

6.—On Double Feasts

s - l - t - T - l - d - t - s - l - s - l - F   f - l - d - d - t - l - s l - t s S

℟. Thánks be to Gód.
[A - men.]

7.—On Double Feasts

. d - t - l - s - s - f - L   d - t - s - l - s - s - f - l - L - R   r - m - f - s - l - s -

℟. Thánks
[A -

- f - m - R   r - m - f - s - l - l - s - l - f l l S

be to Gód.
men.]

8.—On Double Feasts

d - m - f - s - S - l - s - f - S - d - l - s - f - s - l - S   s - m - r - d - f - m r r D

℟. Thánks be to Gód.
[A men.]

9 and 10.—On Feasts of the Blessed Virgin Mary

l - d - r - m - r - d - T - L - d - l - s - l d - r d T - L
℟. Thánks be to Gód.
[A - men.]

11.—On Sundays throughout the Year

m - f - m - r - M - L d - r - m - f - m - r - d - t - l s - l L
℟. Thánks be to Gód.
[A - men.]

12.—On Semi-double Feasts

s l - t - s - r - d - t - l - S - l - s l - t - l l S
℟. Thánks be to Gód.
[A - men.]

13.—On Semi-double Feasts

l - s - l - d - t - S t - l - d - d - l s - l L
℟. Thánks be to Gód.
[A - men.]

14.—Within Octaves not of the B.V.M.

s - l - s - l - s - s - r - s - f - s - f - m - R r - m - f - s - l - l - s f - s S
℟. Thánks be to Gód.
[A - men.]

15.—On Simple Feasts

s - l - d d - t l T
℟. Thánks be to Gód.
[A - men.]

16.—On Ferias throughout the Year

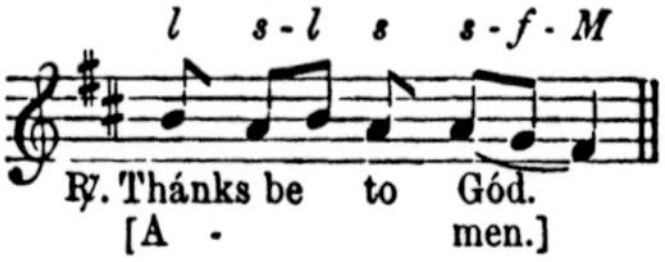
l s - l s s - f - M
℟. Thánks be to Gód.
[A - men.]

17.—On Sundays in Advent and Lent

d - r - f - m - r - d - r - r f - r - M m - f - s - f - m - r - d - r - m - f m R
℟. Thánks be to Gód.
[A - men.]

or the following

d - r - d - r - m s - f - m - r - m - d - t - r - m - r r D
℟. Thánks be to Gód.
[A - men.]

18.—On Ferias in Advent and Lent, on Vigils, and on Ember and Rogation Days

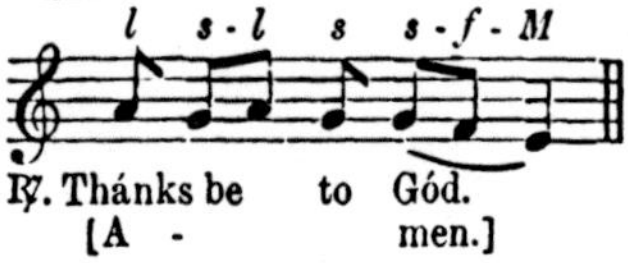
l s - l s s - f - M
℟. Thánks be to Gód.
[A - men.]

Additional Responses

To be used only when the Bishop celebrates

X.—THE CONFESSION TONE

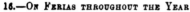

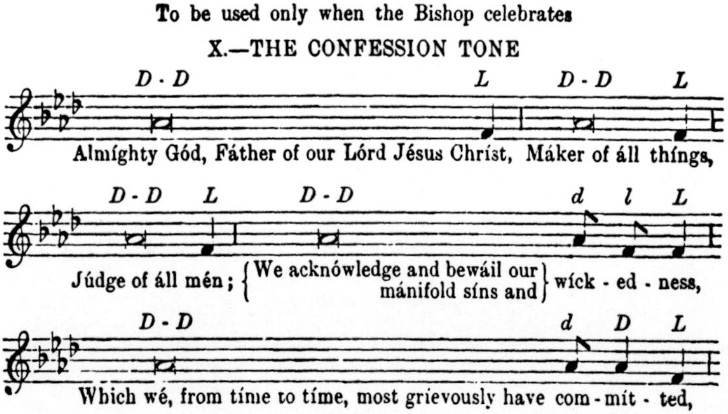
D - D L D - D L
Almíghty Gód, Fáther of our Lórd Jésus Chríst, Máker of áll thíngs,
D - D L D - D d l L
Júdge of áll mén; {We acknówledge and bewáil our mánifold síns and} wíck - ed - ness,
D - D d D L
Which wé, from tíme to tíme, most gríevously have com - mít - ted,

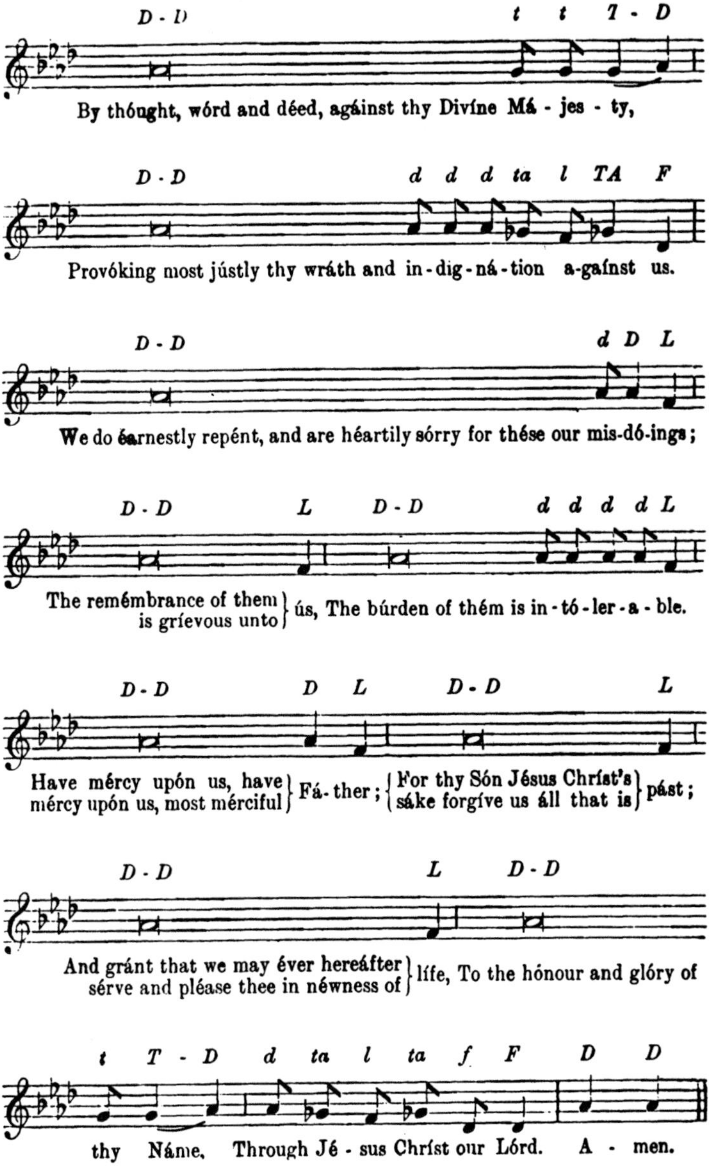
By thóught, wórd and déed, agáinst thy Divíne Má - jes - ty,
Provóking most jústly thy wráth and in - dig - ná - tion a-gaínst us.
We do éarnestly repént, and are héartily sórry for thése our mis-dó-ings;
The remémbrance of them is gríevous unto ús, The búrden of thém is in - tó - ler - a - ble.
Have mércy upón us, have mércy upón us, most mérciful Fá- ther; For thy Són Jésus Chríst's sáke forgíve us áll that is pást;
And gránt that we may éver hereáfter sérve and pléase thee in néwness of lífe, To the hónour and glóry of
thy Náme, Through Jé - sus Chríst our Lórd. A - men.

XI.—THE BISHOP'S BLESSING

℣. Bléss-ed be the Náme of the Lórd. ℟. From thís time fórth for év-er-more.
℣. Our hélp is in the Náme of the Lórd. ℟. Who háth made héaven and éarth.
. . . The bléss-ing of Gód Al-mígh-ty, the Fá-ther, the Són, and the
Hó-ly Ghóst, be a-móngst you and re-máin with you ál-ways. ℟. A-men.

LaVergne, TN USA
25 September 2009

158998LV00003B/4/A

9 780854 021161